Reducing the Time Burdens of Army Company Leaders

LISA SAUM-MANNING, TRACY C. KRUEGER, MATTHEW W. LEWIS,
ERIN N. LEIDY, TETSUHIRO YAMADA, RICK EDEN, ANDREW LEWIS,
ADA L. COTTO, RYAN HABERMAN, ROBERT DION, JR.,
STACY L. MOORE, MICHAEL SHURKIN, MICHAEL LERARIO

 ARROYO CENTER

Prepared for The United States Army
Approved for public release; distribution unlimited

For more information on this publication, visit www.rand.org/t/RR2979

Library of Congress Cataloging-in-Publication Data is available for this publication.
ISBN: 978-1-9774-0350-6

Published by the RAND Corporation, Santa Monica, Calif.
© Copyright 2019 RAND Corporation
RAND® is a registered trademark.

Cover photos (clockwise from top left): Joint Readiness Training Center Public Affairs Office; Staff Sgt. Joaguin Suero; U.S. Army photos by Heather Graham-Ashley, III Corps and Fort Hood Public Affairs; Army.mil/News photo; Cover graphic: Jeffery Hobrath/Getty Images

Support RAND
Make a tax-deductible charitable contribution at
www.rand.org/giving/contribute

www.rand.org

Preface

This report documents research and analysis conducted as part of a project entitled *Analyzing the Effects of Competing Time Demands on Company-Level Leaders*, sponsored by the U.S. Army Forces Command (FORSCOM). The purpose of this project was to analyze alternative approaches that could lead to decreasing the time company-level leaders spend on non–mission-essential tasks so these leaders can focus on the most critical tasks for mission accomplishment and professional development.

This research was conducted within RAND Arroyo Center's Personnel, Training, and Health Program. RAND Arroyo Center, part of the RAND Corporation, is a federally funded research and development center sponsored by the United States Army.

RAND operates under a "Federal-Wide Assurance" (FWA00003425) and complies with the *Code of Federal Regulations for the Protection of Human Subjects Under United States Law* (45 C.F.R. 46), also known as "the Common Rule," as well as with the implementation guidance set forth in the Department of Defense (DoD) Instruction 3216.02. As applicable, this compliance includes reviews and approvals by RAND's Institutional Review Board (the Human Subjects Protection Committee) and by the U.S. Army. The views of sources utilized in this report are solely their own and do not represent the official policy or position of DoD or the U.S. government.

Contents

Figures and Tables

Summary

Company leaders in the Army—company commanders, executive officers, and first sergeants—have long been recognized as overworked. Company leaders implement Army and Department of Defense (DoD) requirements through the careful management of the training and duties of their frontline soldiers. Their jobs are burdensome in part because of the number of requirements imposed on them by higher headquarters. These requirements also include garrison tasks that compete for company leaders' time, such as providing personnel for installation support, participating in community events, and coordinating distinguished visitor visits.

Objective and Approach

The purpose of this report is to help the Army identify ways to reduce and manage the time burdens on Active Component company leaders in garrison. To structure our research, we adopted the Job Demands-Resources (JD-R) model (Bakker and Demerouti, 2014; Demerouti et al., 2001) from the work design literature. The model invites consideration of two levers—job demands and job resources—to address the challenges of reducing time burdens at both organizational and individual worker levels. The model allowed us to conceptualize and organize the problem into three categories for analysis: mitigating job demands through clarity of purpose and task; enhancing job resources with capital improvements to training and resources; and facilitating cultural changes to highlight leaders' awareness of time burdens and improve the productive use of time.

We collected data and information through several methods. We reviewed time-burden issues highlighted in U.S. military literature, including gray literature such as blogs. We also identified best practices in industrial-organizational psychology and business literatures. We conducted focus group discussions at three Army installations with company leaders and interviewed higher-echelon Army leaders, including Army battalion-level leaders. Short surveys were administered during each focus group to collect detailed quantitative information about the demands on company leaders' time.

We also interviewed individuals, both military and civilian, who work in jobs with similar characteristics and time burdens to search broadly for time-management practices that might be applicable to the Army. All interviewees held positions requiring them to lead people and manage resources. We targeted jobs that operate in highly regulated environments, that impose pressure to perform, that have competition for advancement, that contain a service orientation, or that involve physical risk.

The research summarized in this report was conducted before the Secretary of the Army issued a series of Army memos in 2018 removing or reducing a number of mandatory training tasks. Army organizations' approaches to adhering to the intent behind this guidance continue to evolve. The value of this report is in the methodology it outlines, as it provides a framework for understanding a wider range of time burdens impacting soldier readiness and potential solutions for addressing them.

Job Demands Facing Company Leaders

Our survey revealed that company leaders are willing to work long days in garrison; nevertheless, they would like some relief. Survey results indicate company leaders work an average of 12.5-hour workdays. Almost nine out of ten company leaders agree or strongly agree that this time burden makes it difficult to fulfill nonwork responsibilities. The respondents suggest their work-life balance would improve if they average 12 fewer hours per work week—roughly a 53-hour work week, or 10.5 hours per day.

Company leaders allocate their time among many leadership duties and responsibilities as well as core mission tasks. Based on prior research and subject matter experts (SMEs), we identified nine major job demands and asked company leaders to evaluate the approximate time devoted to each major category and what tasks they consider "non–mission-essential." The nine job demands are the following:

- equipment maintenance and accountability
- tracking readiness (personnel and training)
- Army Regulation (AR) 600-20 (Army Command Policy)
- unit-specific training
- higher command—meetings
- higher command—taskings
- AR 350-1 (mandatory Army-wide training)
- installation support
- self-development.

The range of tasks suggests seeking efficiencies in only one or two major job tasks is unlikely to dramatically reduce the total time burden.

Important Job Resources for Company Leaders

In line with the JD-R model and input from SMEs, we identified 11 resources that could help company leaders meet their job demands. In our focus groups, we provided company leaders a list in random order and asked them to evaluate the importance and availability of each resource. They generally judged all their job resources to be moderately or very important. The exception was recognition for one's contributions, either through formal or informal means such as awards or compliments. Below is a list of the 11 job resources:

- delegation
- family support
- command support
- role clarity
- autonomy

- peer support
- formal training
- feedback
- informal mentor
- technology tools
- recognition.

Delegation was rated as very important for enabling task completion, yet about 50 percent of company leaders reported too few delegation resources (defined as soldiers who can effectively meet the leader's intent in completing taskings). Company leaders considered peer support (defined as individuals in similar job positions who contribute to the leader's work performance and/or general well-being) to be moderately important to very important, and approximately 85 percent indicated peer support was "about right."

Company leaders described their technology resources in negative terms (e.g., old, time-consuming to use). However, when asked about the availability of technology tools, approximately half of the company commanders responded there were too many, and the other half responded there were too few.[1] Too many technology tools might refer to the number of systems being utilized to track readiness, whereas too few might refer to insufficient computers at the company level.

Time-Management Strategies That Soldiers Rely on

Soldiers reported using varied strategies to manage their time effectively, but several frequently mentioned strategies appear counterproductive and may lead to suboptimal performance, inaccurate readiness reporting, exhaustion, and burnout. Rather than pushing back on higher command taskings, soldiers may resort to lying, misrepresenting the truth, or seemingly tasking themselves and their subordinates beyond the limits of productivity and effectiveness. Soldiers were

---

[1]   We emphasize this split was only seen among company commanders and not among company first sergeants and company executive officers.

also sometimes reluctant or had difficulty applying some of the more effective approaches. For example, some company leaders preferred not to delegate. Soldiers mentioned prioritization as crucial to task completion. However, some found it difficult to juggle priorities without clearer guidance on higher headquarter priorities. Soldiers indicated following schedules was a useful way to manage time. However, last-minute taskings often make it difficult to schedule effectively. Taskings can arrive at any given time, so no matter how well-planned and seemingly protected a training schedule is, it can be disrupted at the last minute when new requirements take priority.

Solutions Soldiers Would Like Higher Echelons of the Army to Implement

Soldiers proposed a wide variety of solutions to the time-burden problem. These include enhancing technology, creating or restructuring jobs, reducing requirements, improving training, increasing personnel and budgets, providing autonomy, accelerating the removal of noncontributing soldiers, following schedules, and outsourcing some activities. These proposed solutions vary in their feasibility and challenges to implementation. For instance, solutions requiring additional resources, such as personnel and funding, compete with other demands and opportunities for improvement. Other solutions, such as developing and deploying a new information technology system, involve long time frames. Some would require changes at higher levels of the Army—or the "institutional Army."

Solutions Mentioned in Other Domains

Prioritizing tasks was the most frequently mentioned time-management strategy we found outside the Army, followed by delegating tasks to subordinates, and then following schedules. Organizing information (i.e., creating checklists, maintaining calendars) was a commonly cited time-management approach in non-U.S. Army sources but was less popular with company leaders. This difference may be attributed to company leaders lacking adequate administrative skills or tools to think about how best to organize and manage garrison duties.

Recommendations

Given the complex nature of the time-burden challenge for company leaders, implementing any single solution is unlikely to yield much improvement. Substantial change will only come through modifications on many fronts. To substantially reduce the time burden on company leaders the Army will need to implement a variety of time-management strategies concurrently, systematically, and consistently. Using the menu of recommendations we have developed, the Army should develop a sustained, multipronged attack on the time-burden problem. Though progress will be gradual, the Army through a concerted effort can successfully reduce the time burdens on company commanders so their work days are long but not excessively so.

As these results suggest, we found no silver bullet for eliminating the time-burden challenge for company leaders. We did, however, develop specific actions within each of the three categories of recommendations to reduce time burdens on company leaders—clarity of purpose and task, capital improvements to training and resources, and facilitating cultural changes—that may help both the institutional Army and company leaders enable best practices for time management and avoid relying on counterproductive strategies. These recommendations are highlighted in Table S.1.

Our recommendations encompass both actions company leaders can take and those requiring an organizational response from higher levels in the Army. At the organizational level, we identify ways senior leadership might establish conditions that reduce or help manage the inordinate number of company leader's primary duties and responsibilities, garrison-centric tasks, and requirements placed on company leaders. At the individual level, we identify time-management strategies that may help company leaders optimize the limited time available to satisfy mission and training objectives.

Table S.1
High-Level Recommendations to Reduce Time Burdens

Clarity	
Focused on mitigating job demands	
General recommendation	**Example**
• Define and concentrate effort on important tasks; critically screen urgent tasks	• Identify a limited number of priorities
• Timing matters: minimize distractions through consolidation and discipline	• Consolidate required trainings when permitted
• Know the time involved to complete taskings and focus on the meaning associated with metrics (red, amber, green)	• Determine complete time implications of taskings, including time effects on other activities
Capital	
Focused on improving job resources	
General recommendation	**Example**
• Augment access to, compatibility with, and capability of technical systems	• Replace Digital Training Management System (DTMS)
• Enhance formal training and support tools	• Improve teaching of administrative and managerial skills prior to promotion to leadership position
• Increase personnel available to company leaders to support administrative and installation support tasks	• Add Human Resource Specialists, Administrative System Digital Master Gunners[a] and/or DTMS clerks
Culture	
Focused on improving the job environment	
General recommendation	**Example**
• Enforce existing timeline-related doctrine and policy	• Enforce FORSCOM six-week lock-in policy
• Provide autonomy to company leaders	• Accept increased risk with new leaders to provide leader development opportunities
• Encourage pushback based on accurate assessment of current capabilities	• Reward honesty and highlight candor in Officer Evaluation Reports ratings

[a] An Administrative Systems Digital Master Gunner would be a subject matter expert who can configure, operate, maintain and coordinate the connectivity of DTMS or other tracking systems of record. Creating such a position could ease company command staff's administrative burden so they can focus on core Mission Essential Task List (METL) tasks.

Acknowledgments

We would like to thank our sponsors, LTG Laura Richardson, Kirk Palan, and Kristin Blake for their support of this project. We would also like to thank CPT Jason Lee, Terry Walker, and MAJ Justin M. Ducôté for coordinating installation visits; LTC Bradley May, MAJ Crispin J. Burke, and MAJ Ryan Laughna provided additional support and expertise. The document was significantly improved based on the constructive reviews of Susan Straus of RAND and LTG Joe Martz, Retired. Finally, we thank the many military personnel and civilian professionals who shared invaluable insights about their daily workplace environments. This report benefited greatly from their willingness to commit precious and limited time to discuss the types of time-burden challenges they experience; this project would not have been possible without their frankness and candor.

Abbreviations

APFT	Army Physical Fitness Test
AR	Army Regulation
ATUS	American Time Use Survey
BCT	Brigade Combat Team
BMM	borrowed military manpower
BN	battalion
CTG	Commander's Training Guidance
DoD	Department of Defense
DTMS	Digital Training Management System
eMILPO	Electronic Military Personnel Office
EO	equal opportunity
FORSCOM	U.S. Army Forces Command
FRAGO	fragmentary order
GAO	Government Accountability Office
IT	information technology
JD-R	Job Demands-Resources
METL	Mission Essential Task List
NCFA	National Commission on the Future of the Army
NCO	noncommissioned officer
OER	Officer Evaluation Report

PT	physical training
SHARP	Sexual Harassment/Assault Response and Prevention
SME	subject matter expert
SOP	standard operating procedure

CHAPTER ONE

Introduction

Company leaders in the Army face an inherent tension between activities that develop combat readiness and other mandatory training and administrative tasks associated with life in garrison. Leaders must establish priorities based on requirements for fighting the nation's wars, yet their days are often consumed by miscellaneous support tasks that can distract them from their primary roles and responsibilities. These distractions may also affect their own leadership development and advancement.

The Army is aware of the potentially excessive time demands placed on its company leaders. For example, a 2002 Army War College study found the days required to complete all mandatory training directives "literally exceeds the number of training days available to company commanders. Company commanders somehow have to fit 297 days of mandatory requirements into 256 available training days" (Wong, 2002, pp. 8–9). A 2015 Army G-3/5/7 study described "an unacceptable level of friction" between balancing training readiness with other Army requirements competing for unit time (U.S. Department of the Army, G-3/5/7 Staff, 2015). In 2016, the National Commission on the Future of the Army (NCFA) identified "over 1,000 Army directives, regulations, pamphlets, and messages [addressing] mandatory training" and recommended the Army "reduce mandatory training prescribed in AR 350-1 [Army Regulation 350-1, *Army Training and Leader Development*]" (NCFA, 2016, p. 77). As the U.S. Army Forces Command (FORSCOM) 2018 Command Training Guidance acknowledges, "The number one resource constraint reflected by unit commanders is the lack of available time. We have many requirements and not enough time to accomplish them to standard" (U.S. Army Forces Command, 2017, p. 2).

Our literature reviews and discussions with junior leaders reveal a general perception that, while considered important, General Military Training such as Suicide Prevention, Resilience, Cybersecurity, and Equal Opportunity contribute to overtasking. These requirements across the Department of Defense (DOD) do not include Army-specific training requirements such as Army Command Policy AR 600-20) responsibilities pertaining to health, fitness, and morale and award ceremony attendance or to garrison tasks such as providing personnel for installation support, participating in community events, and coordinating distinguished guest visits. With so many requirements and taskings to satisfy and not enough time to complete them, it has long been "commonplace for military leaders to call a company commander's job the hardest job in the Army" (Meyer, 1990). Additionally, as one critic points out, with the wars in Iraq and Afghanistan largely drawn to a close, a largely garrisoned Army will continue to confront company commanders "with the crush of requirements (training and administrative) mandated by higher headquarters" ("Building Combat Ready Teams: The Crush of Requirements from Higher Headquarters," 2012).

The Secretary of the Army recently took steps to address the problem, starting with a series of five memorandums published in April–June 2018 eliminating the following mandatory training requirements:

1. Travel Risk Planning System
2. Media Awareness Training
3. Combatting Trafficking in Persons
4. Accident Avoidance Course Training (AR 600-55)
5. Grade Requirements for Additional Duty Safety Officer (AR 385-10)
6. Internal audits of dining facility headcounts (AR 600-38)
7. Culture, regional expertise, and language training (AR 350-1)
8. Code of Conduct, Personnel Recovery, or Survival Escape Resistance and Evasion Level-A (AR 350-1, AR 525-28)

9. Semiannual Tool Room inventory requirement (AR 710-2)
10. Multisource Assessment and Feedback (AR 600-100)
11. Privately owned vehicle inspections prior to long weekends or holidays
12. Transgender training, as it is complete across the Army, and units no longer need to report training status
13. Substance abuse prevention training
14. Human Relations Readiness Training (AR 600-20).

Reducing mandatory training requirements may help reduce the administrative burden on company leaders who must spend valuable time tracking their soldiers' compliance.[1] However, other actions are also needed to help leaders better manage the time they have. For example, a February 2016 Army Directive instituted a policy to reduce disruptions to training schedules:

> [T]he Army will "lock out" external taskings that affect the training schedule of brigades and their subordinate units six weeks before scheduled training for the Active Component (company level) and 13 weeks before scheduled training for the Reserve Component (company level). (Army Directive 2016-05, 2016, p. 1)

The time-burden challenge is rooted in the depths of an Army culture that continually tasks soldiers—rather than asking whether company leaders realistically have the time and resources to accomplish all the tasks. Many of the same burdens reported in this study also occur with Reserve Component company leaders, who have different but significant constraints on the time available to meet competing demands. However, this study focused solely on the Active Component.

---

[1] Company leaders manage numerous reporting requirements submitted by their soldiers. For example, until June 2018, leaders were responsible for tracking subordinates' travel risk assessments and motor vehicle accident records among other information not directly associated with their unit's core mission.

Research Purpose and Approach

The purpose of this report is to better understand the time burdens facing company leaders and identify potential solutions to overcome them. We focused on exploring demands, resources, and solutions from sources including focus groups and one-on-one interviews. To structure our research, we adopted the Job Demands-Resources (JD-R) model (Bakker and Demerouti, 2014) from the work design literature and applied core components to the current problem set and solution strategies.[2] Specifically, for this report, the model provides a flexible and comprehensive conceptual framework dividing work environments between job demands and job resources. Job demands are work activities requiring sustained physical or psychological effort, whereas job resources contribute to achieving goals, reducing demands, or facilitating personal growth. Thus, the JD-R model invites consideration of two levers—demands and resources—to address the challenges of reducing time burdens.

Additionally, the model suggests these levers can be used at both the organizational level, characterized as "job redesign" and the individual worker level described as "job crafting" (see Table 1.1). This approach allowed us to identify actions the Army (at the organizational level) could pursue to reduce the time burden of company lead-

---

[2]   Building on the demand-control model (R. A. Karasek, "Job Demands, Job Decision Latitude, and Mental Strain: Implications for Job Redesign," *Administrative Science Quarterly*, Vol. 24, 1979, pp. 285–308), the JD-R model was originally developed to explain burnout in the workplace (Evangelia Demerouti et al., "The Job Demands-Resources Model of Burnout," *Journal of Applied Psychology*, Vol. 86, 2001, pp. 499–512). The JD-R model has since been expanded and now outlines several predictions about employee well-being (e.g., engagement, burnout) and performance based on the demands and resources of a job (for more complete discussions, see Arnold B. Bakker and Evangelia Demerouti, "Job Demands-Resources Theory," in Peter Y. Chen and Cary L. Cooper, eds., *Work and Wellbeing*, Vol. III: *Wellbeing: A Complete Reference Guide*, Hoboken, N.J.: Wiley, 2014; W. B. Schaufeli and Toon W. Taris, "A Critical Review of the Job Demands-Resources Model: Implications for Improving Work and Health," in G. F. Bauer and O. Hämmig, eds., *Bridging Occupational, Organizational and Public Health: A Transdisciplinary Approach*, Dordrecht, the Netherlands: Springer, 2014, pp. 43–68). Given the scope of our effort, we do not expand on important nuances such as the difference between job resources and personal resources, which are defined as an individual's perspective of his or her ability to control the environment.

ers (Grant and Parker, 2009) as well as practices company leaders (at the individual level) could adopt to improve management of burdens (Wrzesniewski and Dutton, 2001).

Table 1.1 identifies, defines, and provides examples of the core components we leveraged from the JD-R model to frame the current problem set and solution strategies. These four components—demands,

Table 1.1
Project Framework: Time-Burden Problems and Solutions

Component	Definition	Examples
Problem set		
Demands[a]	Aspects of the job that require physical and/or psychological effort.	"Hindrance" • Administrative hassles • Role ambiguity "Challenge" • Responsibility
Resources	Aspects of the job that (a) help achieve work goals, (b) reduce job demands, or (c) stimulate personal growth, learning, and development.	• Support • Autonomy
Solution strategies		
Redesign *(organization)*	A top-down approach in which the organization or the supervisor makes a structural modification to something about the job, task, or conditions of the individual.	• Add a job position • Reduce work tasks
Crafting *(individual)*	Efforts initiated by the individual to actively change the job (e.g., selecting which tasks to pursue, choosing who to work with, and modifying the way they think about tasks).	• Prioritize tasks • Determine task completion method

[a] Although the term "demands" can have a negative connotation, job demands can be both "bad" and "good" from the perspective of the worker (see Marcie A. Cavanaugh et al., "An Empirical Examination of Self-Reported Work Stress Among U.S. Managers," *Journal of Applied Psychology*, Vol. 85, No. 1, 2000, pp. 65–74). Hindrance demands—such as administrative hassles and role ambiguity—are negatively associated with engagement; alternatively, challenge demands—such as responsibility—are positively associated with engagement (see Eean R. Crawford, Jeffery A. LePine, and Bruce Louis Rich, "Linking Job Demands and Resources to Employee Engagement and Burnout: A Theoretical Extension and Meta-Analytic Test," *Journal of Applied Psychology*, Vol. 95, No. 5, 2010, pp. 834–848).

resources, organizational redesign, and individual crafting—guided the design of our data collection and analyses.

Following the project framework, our research team took a multipronged approach. We focused on exploring the problems (demands, resources) and solutions from both military and nonmilitary sources using several methods, including literature reviews, paper surveys, and semistructured discussions (focus groups and one-on-one interviews) (see Figure 1.1).

Including nonmilitary perspectives was critical to this effort. The challenge of "too much to do and not enough time" is shared by many hardworking individuals: one in four American workers report they do not feel as though they have enough time to do their jobs, and about half report working during their free (unpaid) time to meet job expectations (Maestas et al., 2017). Although the specific demands,

Figure 1.1
Methods and Sources to Gather Information About Time Burdens and Solutions

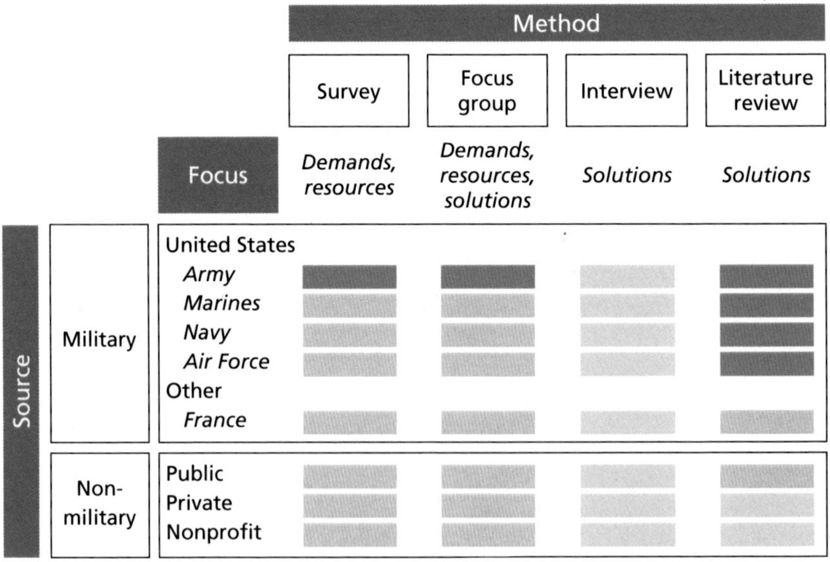

			Method			
		Focus	Survey	Focus group	Interview	Literature review
			Demands, resources	Demands, resources, solutions	Solutions	Solutions
Source	Military	United States				
		Army				
		Marines				
		Navy				
		Air Force				
		Other				
		France				
	Non-military	Public				
		Private				
		Nonprofit				

NOTE: Dark green indicates a primary focus; light green indicates a secondary focus; gray indicates not included.

resources, and context of nonmilitary jobs may differ from those of company leaders, solutions developed outside the Army might be applicable.

Participation of 120 Soldiers in Surveys and Focus Groups

We used surveys and focus groups with soldiers to gain an appreciation for the type and amount of demands associated with certain positions to determine the importance and availability of resources, and to learn about solutions for both the organization and individual to adopt. We conducted 1.5-hour focus groups with company leaders at the three Army Corps locations: (I Corps [Joint Base Lewis-McChord], III Corps [Fort Hood], and XVIII Corps [Fort Bragg]) representing five job positions (company commanders, executive officers, and first sergeants), as well as platoon leaders and platoon sergeants across many different company types (e.g., Infantry, Armor, Aviation, Field Artillery), although the emphasis was on companies within Brigade Combat Teams (BCTs).[3]

Short surveys were administered during each focus group (see Appendix for the survey). The survey sought quantitative information about the nature of time demands on company leaders to include how many hours individuals are working and what percentage of their time is devoted to each of the nine major task groupings identified through discussions with Army subject matter experts (SMEs), such as Equipment Maintenance and Accountability, AR 350-1 (Mandatory Army-Wide Training), and Unit-Specific Training. Figure 1.2 provides demographic information about our survey and focus group participants.

---

[3] Focus group participation was voluntary and requested through a FORSCOM-issued fragmentary order (FRAGO) submitted to the three installations. While many units received the order, it is not possible to determine participation rates as the exact number of soldiers who received the participation request is unknown. Many others, who were likely busy with multiple other taskings along the lines of those described in this report, could have provided additional information not covered in our discussions.

Figure 1.2
Characteristics of Focus Group Participants

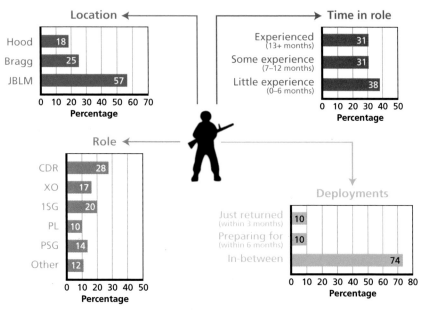

NOTE: For role, results sum greater than 100 percent due to rounding. For deployment status, seven participants did not indicate a response.

JBLM indicates Joint Base Lewis-McChord. 1SG = first sergeant; CDR = commander; PL = platoon leader; PSG = platoon sergeant; and XO = executive officer.

The analysis of soldiers' responses helped us understand the context of the time-burden challenge so we could better focus our search for potential solutions.

We Reviewed Three Distinct Literatures and Interviewed 69 Professionals

The purpose of our literature review and interviews with professionals outside the Army was to explore broadly for relevant solutions. We searched both peer-reviewed sources as well as the gray literature, such as blogs. Over 170 articles were identified as potentially relevant and were examined more closely. The reviews did not focus on identifying sources or consequences of time burdens, although this information is often associated with solutions. Prior to searching, we created a list of keywords specific to each sector that might yield relevant articles. For example, we identified and applied 61 search terms from the military literature review such as "time management," "do more with less," and "mandatory fun." The number of articles identified and the sources searched are the following:

- military literature (77 articles): Military database, Rally Point, *Small Wars Journal*, U.S. Naval Institute Blog, War on the Rocks, and Duffle Blog
- private literature (46 articles): *Harvard Business Review, Forbes, Entrepreneur, Fortune,* and *Inc.*
- nonprofit literature (53 articles): PsychARTICLES, PsychINFO, and Web of Science.

The one-hour phone interviews followed the same structure as our focus groups. These interviews varied from one-on-one conversations to several individuals in a group discussion. To increase the likelihood the solutions identified in this effort would be applicable to our target population, we selected interviewees from professions sharing at least some similarities with company leaders' jobs and the context in which they work.[4] Therefore, all interviewees held positions in which they were required to lead people and manage resources. Additionally, we targeted jobs that operate in highly regulated environments, apply pressure to perform, have competition for advancement, contain a service orientation, or involve physical risk. Figure 1.3 presents the number and type of interviewees.

---

[4] We relied on an internal network of RAND SMEs to identify potential interview candidates in the professions of interest. We also used the snowball technique, asking interviewees for additional points of contact within their fields who may be interested in sharing their time management best practices. Thirty-six of the 40 individuals we contacted agreed to be interviewed—a 90-percent participation rate.

Figure 1.3
Professions of the 69 Interviewees

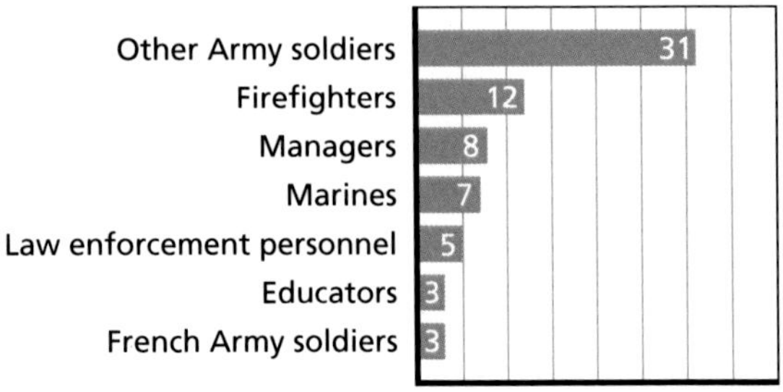

Organization of the Report

In the following chapters, we present the findings of our analysis and recommendations for action. Chapter Two contains our analysis of current job burdens borne by company leaders and their assessment of the importance of various resources for managing these burdens. Chapter Three focuses on identifying time-management or other burden-lifting strategies currently used by company leaders, on potential solutions they would like to see the Army implement at higher organizational levels, and on a comparison with approaches discovered in the time-management literature. Chapter Four presents our recommendations. Chapter Five concludes with a summary of the findings and a few thoughts on potential areas of future research.

CHAPTER TWO

Company Leaders' Job Demands and Resources

The research team traveled to three military installations—Joint Base Lewis-McChord, Fort Hood, and Fort Bragg—to conduct 1.5-hour focus groups. During each discussion, we administered a short survey to collect quantitative data, to ensure all attendees participated, and to structure the group discussion. In line with the framing described in Chapter One (i.e., the core components of the JD-R model), this chapter presents soldiers' results evaluating various features of the "problem set," which we define as job demands and resources. Although we conducted focus groups with 120 soldiers, the data presented in this chapter are limited to the responses from 77 company leaders: company commanders (n = 33), executive officers (n = 20), and first sergeants (n = 24). We begin by presenting data evaluating job demands to include the amount of time estimated to meet these demands and an evaluation of whether they are non–mission-essential.[1] Next, we report company leaders' assessment of the importance and availability of job resources for managing those burdens.

Job Demands Facing Company Leaders

To understand the amount of time company leaders devote to their work, we asked: "Think back to YESTERDAY; how long did you work

---

[1] We use the term "non–mission-essential" to distinguish between tasks outlined in a unit's mission essential task list (METL) and tasks that may enhance the primary mission but are outside the unit's core mission.

Figure 2.1
The Company Command Team Worked Approximately 12.5 Hours "Yesterday," Including Physical Training and Work at Home

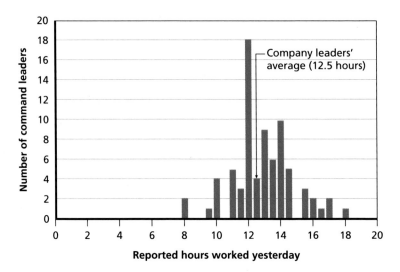

(including physical training and evenings)?" Survey results indicate company leaders work an average of 12.5 hours a day (see Figure 2.1). In contrast, data from the 2014 American Time Use Survey (ATUS) show that, of the 44 percent of Americans engaging in working or work-related activities, only about 4 percent work 12.5 hours or more (see Figure 2.2).[2] Further, almost nine out of ten company leaders agree or strongly agree the time demands of their job make it difficult to fulfill nonwork responsibilities (e.g., home, family, social). Company leaders indicate they could improve their work-life balance if they aver-

---

[2]   The Bureau of Labor Statistics conducts the ATUS annually and uses a similar "yester-day" question format when asking about how individuals spend their time. It is important to note that these data do not include physical training which is a work requirement factored into soldier work days. The ATUS includes residents age 15 and older in U.S. households, except for active military personnel and individuals in nursing homes and prisons. The ATUS uses a stratified sample based on (1) race/ethnicity of the householder, (2) presence and age of children, and (3) number of adults in adults-only households. These data include part-time and full-time workers. In 2014, the response rate was 51 percent. See U.S. Census Bureau, *American Time Use Survey User's Guide: Understanding ATUS 2003 to 2017*, Washington, D.C.: Bureau of Labor Statistics, June 2018.

Figure 2.2
Only About 4 Percent of Working Civilians Worked 12.5 Hours or More "Yesterday"

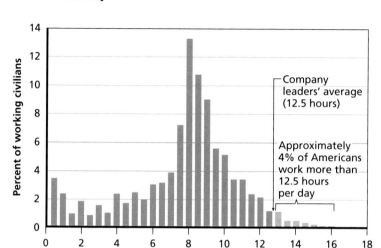

SOURCE: Yau (*FlowingData*, undated) used data from the 2014 ATUS.
NOTE: The combination of the purple bars totals approximately 96 percent.

age 12 fewer work hours per week. Based on other data we collected, this desired reduction translates to about a 53-hour work week, or 10.5 hours a day. In comparison, the ATUS indicates only about 13 percent of individuals report working that long or longer.

We also sought to understand what types of tasks compete for these long working hours. To provide focus group participants with a common frame-of-reference to discuss job demands, we presented nine major task categories in random order (such as Equipment Maintenance/Accountability and Unit-Specific Training) and specific examples of each (see Appendix for the survey).[3] Figure 2.3 shows the estimated percentage of time per quarter company leaders devote personally (as opposed to their subordinate soldiers) to each of the nine major job tasks as well as which tasks respondents consider "non–

---

[3] The major task categories were determined based on iterative Army SME input.

Figure 2.3
Company Leaders' Estimates of Job Task Allocations

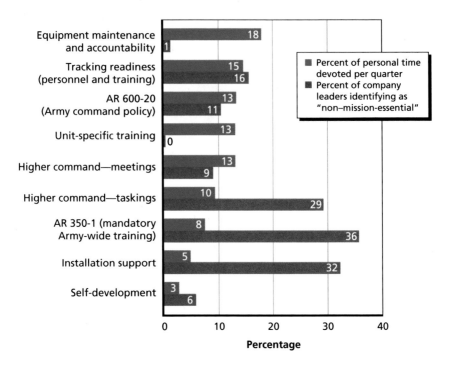

mission-essential" at their respective echelon.[4] The intent of these questions was to gain a general sense of company leaders' perception of time use and noncriticality.

These data suggest company leaders allocate their working hours among a wide range of activities. For example, one company leader observed:

> There are so many different things that you have to track and do. You are constantly playing Whack-a-Mole. If you are good on something then you are jacked-up on something else. Or maybe I am just not a good commander. It just compounds (e.g., brigade is

---

[4] During administration, we emphasized that we were only interested in their time as leaders, not their unit's time.

reacting to division). Go do this and go do that. The people that pay the tax on this is the junior enlisted, they just have to eat it.

Even AR 350-1 (Mandatory Army-Wide Training)—the task respondents most frequently identified as "non–mission-essential"—only averaged 8 percent of company leaders' time per quarter.[5] The range of tasks suggests seeking efficiencies in only one or two job tasks is unlikely to dramatically reduce the total time burden. This conclusion is highlighted in Figure 2.4, with an emphasis on the time spent in training-related activities. Although many leaders in the Army are aware and often focus on the time burdens from training, they estimate training takes up just 21 percent of their time during a quarter.

Figure 2.4
Company Leaders' Estimates of Personal Time Devoted Per Quarter to Job Tasks

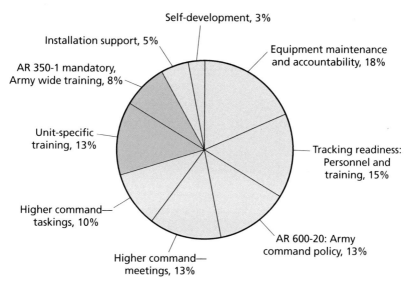

NOTE: Sections highlighted are training-related tasks and sum to 21 percent of estimated time per quarter.

---

[5] Our findings support previous studies that have reviewed the number and types of general military training requirements levied on military personnel. A 2012 RAND study found that general military training accounted for less than 1 percent of available training time for

During focus groups, soldiers also referenced the unacknowledged or "shadow" time required to execute seemingly straightforward tasks. Even capstone activities of short duration can easily hollow out a unit by requiring additional hours, days, and sometimes weeks of preparation.

> Battalion and above have no visibility of what we are doing and what that takes. They are incredibly disconnected; they grew up in a different era. Take a visual Stryker display for some school district. It is just an hour tasking [for eight soldiers], but it's a lot more prep work than that. It's a four-day build-up. You have to take the floor boards in and out, take it to the wash rack, make sure the weapons systems are straight, etc. Or let's say a $100,000 tent was broken. The leaders that grew up in Iraq and Afghanistan used to be able to just buy a new tent, and it would be here next week. Now we have to go through a process and it takes time. Senior leaders see taskings across the boards but don't see the build-up.

> When brigade requires company commanders for meetings and they don't see others' requirements from division. It's always just the last thing that breaks the camel's back.

Resource Importance and Availability to Company Leaders

We also asked focus group participants to rate the importance and availability of 11 job resources.[6] The list was derived from resources

---

Active Duty personnel across the services (Roland J. Yardley et al., *General Military Training: Standardization and Reduction Options*, Santa Monica, Calif.: RAND Corporation, TR-1222-OSD, 2012, p. xv). A 2017 Government Accountability Office (GAO) report cited estimates from service officials that, "it would take an individual less than 20 hours to complete all common military training requirements" (Cary B. Russell, *DOD Training: DOD Has Taken Steps to Assess Common Military Training*, Washington, D.C.: U.S. Government Accountability Office, GAO-17-468, 2017).

[6] Resources were initially identified from the JD-R model and then modified with Army SME input.

commonly identified in the literature and categorized into three broad themes

- support: informal mentorship, command support, peer support, delegation, family support
- enablers: technology tools, formal training, role clarity, autonomy
- reinforcement: recognition, performance feedback.

Company leaders generally judged their resources to be moderately or very important. The exception was recognition—defined as being recognized for one's contributions, either through formal or informal means such as awards or compliments. Judgments of the availability of each resource type fell between "too little" and "about right." The results are presented in Figure 2.5.

Figure 2.5
All Company Leaders Consider Delegation Important, Yet 50 Percent Report Too Little

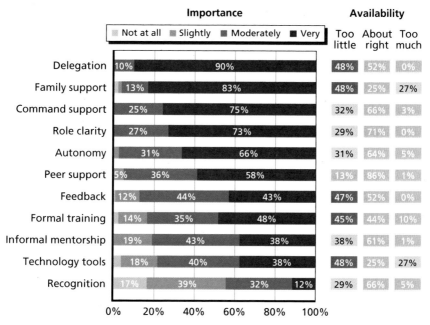

NOTE: Light red indicates a share between 25–45 percent, and dark red indicates a share 45 percent or greater.

Key highlights of the data on the importance and availability of the rated resources include the following:

- Delegation was rated as a very important resource to enable task completion, yet 48 percent of company leaders reported too few delegation resources (defined as soldiers who can effectively meet the leader's intent in completing taskings).
- Peer support (defined as individuals in similar job positions who contribute to the leader's work performance and/or general well-being) was viewed as moderately important to very important to company-level leaders. Approximately 86 percent of company leaders indicated peer support was about right.
- Feedback was viewed as more than moderately important, yet 47 percent of company commanders indicated they have too little regular and constructive feedback about their performance.

Company leaders had conflicting perceptions of the availability of technology tools: 48 percent reported having too little and 27 percent reported having too much. This range may reflect the variety of technology tools that could be subsumed in this category. For example, focus group participants described some technology tools as "old and way behind [with] buttons falling off the computers." Others noted a general lack of adequate accessibility. As one platoon sergeant explained, "I have 90 people and only three computers." In contrast, other focus group participants believed technological advances have allowed the Army to infiltrate their daily lives beyond reasonable limits:

> When you are getting phone calls every time you try to go to a family event, that's mostly the problem. You're never left alone. I get more emails at 8 pm about the duty tomorrow. Why the hell are you bothering me at home at 2200 at night? . . . My phone has rung 17 times since we've been in this discussion!

For many American workers, including soldiers, access to an individual computer is associated with typical working conditions. Our discussions, however, indicate the assumption is unwarranted in Army companies. The current solution to this material shortfall is either use personal computers or go to a library and wait in line.

My office has two computers for 42 people. And one computer belongs to the LT [lieutenant]. And everyone wants something online.

Technology tools. It's fine that the Army is trying to do online, digital training, but most platoons with 30–40 guys have two computers. We have more computers available, but we don't have enough internet drops. The IT [information technology] infrastructure doesn't support the mission. It's not wireless, it's antiquated. We should do more online, sending leave forms through the internet.

I'm using a laptop that's the same one I had in high school. The fact is that our computers are ancient, [and] the internet goes out. It might be unit-specific; other units may have it better. We as an Army are falling behind on the technology. I have one computer for the platoon to do training, but it's the one I'm also using.

Others expressed frustrations with the overreliance on computer-based products for communicating issues pertaining to unit readiness. Although PowerPoint briefings can help commanders visualize areas of progress and those needing improvement, focus group participants noted spending an inordinate amount of time on aesthetic qualities rather than substantive content.

When the Army went to PowerPoints, it was a great tool in the beginning. But now it's about making the slides look pretty so it doesn't distract the senior person in the room. PowerPoint has taken away from being an officer. You take more time in making slides look pretty than the actual plan. For instance, when you are briefing a CONOP [concept of operation], it has a picture and timeline and all that other stuff, and sometimes you get feedback about the font rather than that mission is going to fail because you don't have ammo. Yes, that is a great range, but you don't have ammo. PowerPoint distracts. It's all about PowerPoint.

In the next chapter, we provide an overview of soldiers' strategies for managing time burdens, supplemented with observations from the broader literature on how organizations cope with time-management challenges.

CHAPTER THREE
Strategies for Managing Time Burdens

This chapter focuses on strategies used by all soldiers, not just company leaders, for managing time burdens. We asked all participants in the 120 focus groups which job-crafting strategies they use most frequently and what potential solutions they would like the Army to implement at higher organizational levels. To offer additional perspective on the strategies the soldiers recommended, we also turned to the research literature on time management to compare how frequently such strategies are used and to explore their potential effectiveness.

Solutions Soldiers Frequently Implement

We sought a better understanding of how soldiers currently solve the time-burden challenge. Through an iterative process, we coded data acquired from our semistructured discussions and literature reviews (approximately 1,400 excerpts) to identify and refine 36 Army-level time-management strategies and 31 individual-level strategies. In the following sections, we first review specific time-management strategies frequently discussed in our Army focus groups and then compare them with strategies frequently mentioned in other domains we searched. We then characterized these strategies as effective or counterproductive, based on the literature and discussions with Army SMEs. Table 3.1 presents strategies, descriptions, and examples of the most frequently implemented solutions discussed in our Army focus groups.

Although soldiers mentioned many solutions for managing their time effectively, several top solutions appeared to be counterproductive

Table 3.1
Time-Management Approaches Most Frequently Used by Soldiers

Strategy	Description	Examples
Counterproductive		
Just do it	Company leaders demonstrate a "can-do" attitude, characteristic of the Army, and may involve strategies such as staying late, arriving early, and/or "satisficing" (i.e., good enough).	• "You do what you have to do to accomplish the task, but you do not put [in] the effort that you would like to." • "My last company figured it out. One Digital Training Management System (DTMS) operator worked overnight, 1800–0600, to make sure the info is up."
Lie	Company leaders intentionally falsify information such as reporting an activity is completed when it is not. This includes instances when completion is anticipated soon.	• "Lie constantly." • "You make the bubbles green."[a] • "You want numbers, I can give you numbers." • "I know you're on terminal leave, but if anyone asks, you're good to go."
Misrepresent	Company leaders distort what was done in some way such as oversimplifying or shortening the activity.	• "Nobody does the online training. We click through things. We don't have time. Whatever they think is happening, it's not."
Effective		
Delegate	Company leaders assign tasks and/or roles to others for completion.	• "You have to delegate. As a PL [platoon leader], you can do it all yourself. At the CO [commanding officer] level, you can't—unless you are here until 2100 every night. I focus on what I have to do as a company commander."
Prioritize	Company leaders determine which tasks to complete based on some criteria such as importance or duration (also referred to as planning).	• "You need to know the difference between rubber balls, wood balls, and glass balls. Our job is to keep the glass balls from falling." • "It all depends. If it's anything specific to a person, I won't waste any of my dudes' times. If it has to do with a soldier and/or his family or training, then it goes to the top." • "The phrase we hear is that 'something has to fail.' The one I won't do is often the one that I can articulate best why I'm not doing it. Or what am I going to get chewed-out for less? Where is the least amount of pain?"

Table 3.1—Continued

Strategy	Description	Examples
Follow schedules	Company leaders enforce predetermined agendas, timetables, and so on.	• "I try to keep a routine such as a company meeting every Friday or check metrics every Monday. This routine keeps things on the radar; even if they are messed up, at least we have a plan."
CO	Company leaders pursue feedback, mentorship, and additional learning opportunities from others (including peers, leaders, etc.).	• "I reached out to peers or counterparts at other sites to find best practices."

[a] "Making the bubbles green" refers to the red-yellow-green stoplight chart frequently used to depict unit readiness status. Green would assess a unit as proficient in a given task.

(categorized as "just do it," "lie," and "misrepresent") and can lead to inaccurate readiness reporting. For example, faced with multiple competing tasks, soldiers mentioned at times being exhausted beyond the point of productivity but having to "just do it" without regard for how well they actually accomplish the task. As one company commander explained, "You do what you have to do to accomplish the task, but not put the effort you would like to because we have 4–5 things stacking up that you have to do."

For ease of tracking and communication, many complicated and important activities are summarized by a simple evaluation of "green," "yellow," or "red." This stoplight presentation, theoretically, should act as an indicator to spark thoughtful discussion as to why a given area might be yellow or red and what future actions should be taken to remedy the issue, if it needs addressing now. However, it appears the focus is on the evaluation itself and not what it signifies, which prevents important conversations from taking place. As one soldier stated,

It's all about stats. The real question is, are we good at our job? All of these mindless metrics don't help. It should be about if the company is good at what we do—go find and kill the enemy.

Instead, the focus is on if all of your stats are green. There is [a] zero defect mentality. If someone is delinquent then you are bad at your job. We are lying to ourselves. I say I am truthful and you are considered bad and so we have normalized it—"Yeah we are good." They say green . . . good to go. If I have one overdue then it is the end of the world, so you might as well make green.

A 2015 *Army Times* article described how soldiers misrepresent their mandatory training statistics:

We needed to get SHARP [Sexual Harassment/Assault Response and Prevention] training done and reported to higher headquarters, so we called the platoons and told them to gather the boys around the radio and we said, "Don't touch girls." A nine-man squad pressed for time to complete a mandatory online course "would pick the smartest dude, and he would go in and take it nine times for the other members . . . and then that way they had a certificate to prove that they had completed it." (Lilley, 2015)

The outcome of such strategies is not limited to inaccurate readiness reporting. Research suggests conflict among one's roles is associated with burnout (Lee and Ashforth, 1996). In this case, the act of misrepresenting numbers to achieve training objectives conflicts with the responsibility of complying with rules and policies. Further, it has been suggested that engaging in counterproductive work behaviors can subsequently create a stressful work environment, which further perpetuates engagement in counterproductive work behaviors (Meier and Spector, 2013). Thus, while soldiers may be able to utilize these solutions temporarily, in the long run these solutions are likely to be detrimental to individual soldiers as well as the Army at large.

Soldiers were also sometimes reluctant to apply the more effective approaches or had difficulty doing so. For example, some soldiers preferred not to delegate (a key component of mission command that commanders at all echelons are encouraged to practice). One reason may be that a downsizing military has increased promotion pressures and driven a "zero defect" mentality, leading soldiers to take on more tasks that they would normally trust others to perform. Another reason might be company commanders' lacking the experience to identify the strengths and weaknesses of their soldiers to have confidence in their soldiers' abilities to perform certain tasks. Still another reason is a lack of available personnel to shift some of their daily duties.

> Delegation is important. Great NCOs [noncommissioned officers] are some of the best leaders I've met, and if they aren't doing things it's because they are limited in what they can do. Soldiers [who are] sent off on one tasking keeps the NCOs from doing other important things. We always find a way to get things done, but it always costs time.

Soldiers mentioned prioritization as crucial to task completion. However, some found it difficult to juggle priorities without clearer guidance on higher headquarter priorities.

> Nobody tells the company commander where they can accept risk.

> Role clarity is really important. . . . Do I work for XO [executive officer]? The battalion commander? I don't know who I am working for.

> I really want to know what my brigade commander wants and I don't know what he wants. I would love to talk to him. Our battalion commander is out so it makes my job very challenging.

Soldiers indicated following schedules was a useful way to manage time. However, last-minute taskings often make it difficult to schedule effectively. Taskings can arrive at any time, so no matter how well planned and seemingly protected a training schedule is, it can be disrupted suddenly when new requirements take priority.

> Even though [soldiers] don't always know what is going on, they are still motivated so it motivates me. It's frustrating as a leader because you know they are looking at you like "why didn't you know about this [last-minute task]?" They will do whatever needs to be done. I don't think you get that outside of the military.

Solutions Soldiers Would Like Higher Echelons of the Army to Implement

Soldiers proposed a wide variety of solutions to the time-burden problem that higher echelons of the Army could implement. As shown in Table 3.2, these include organizational-level or redesign-centric solutions such as enhancing technology, creating or restructuring jobs, reducing requirements, improving training, increasing personnel and budgets, providing autonomy, accelerating the removal of noncontributing soldiers, following schedules, and outsourcing some activities. These proposed solutions varied in their feasibility and challenges to implementation. For instance, solutions requiring additional resources, such as personnel and funding, compete with other demands and opportunities for improvement. Other solutions are challenged by long time frames, such as developing and deploying a new IT system. Some would require changes at higher levels of the Army.

Notable among the solutions mentioned was a desire for clearer instructions about priorities. Company leaders receive many signals that some tasks are important, but the volume of inputs combined with their fluctuating emphasis is problematic. These difficulties were widely cited among company leaders expressing a desire for more clarity from higher organizational levels in the Army:

> There needs to be more prioritization at higher levels. Everything is a priority, but that means nothing is a priority. At least that is how it seems. It's just what is the flavor of the day or week? And that is what you must get after that day. It rotates and you just keep up with what you can.

> Hopefully you can read minds. For example, my tingly senses are saying that a weapons qualification is coming up, so I start preparing.

> It's death by a thousand cuts. If you look at a particular battalion, they don't burden us too much, but when you add brigade doing their own initiatives, and then when you stack that upon the division echelons, it gets to be a lot.

Table 3.2
Higher-Echelon Army Solutions Most Frequently Proposed by Soldiers

Theme	Description	Examples
Enhance technology	Implement technical systems with better user interfaces, outputs, and Army-wide compatibility.	• "DTMS is archaic, illogical, crashes all the time. If the Army valued our time they would fix that system."
Create/ restructure jobs	Make structural changes such as developing specialized positions or allowing for flextime and career stability.	• "Borrowed military manpower[a] is criminal. If it is critical then man it. Assign it. Have it in the MTOE." • "Need an MTOE authorized DTMS clerk."
Reduce requirements	Decrease the number of requirements, taskings, and other requests levied on the company.	• "Consolidate 350-1 training. Not all of it is that important. All of it is reactionary." • "No offense, it's things like this right here [the focus group]. It may seem like an hour or two, but it adds up." • "Focus on the amount of taskings that come down from higher. Battalion (BN) has requirements for companies, BDE has requirements for BNs, it all filters down to company level."
Improve training	Enhance the quality of training across the Army (e.g., utilize training professionals, provide cross-training opportunities, increase content relevancy).	• "BOLC taught me to be an engineer but not a leader. Train us [in] ways to manage people and talk with soldiers; what do you say when they have ended their career with a DUI? Handling things at the personal level is all OJT." • "Online training is just checking boxes. If you put it online that means that you don't care about it. If it was face-to-face and a COL has to sit here, then the Army finds it important."
Increase assets	Dedicate more money and manpower to companies.	• "It's about personnel, 80 percent is acceptable manning, which really means we are at 65 percent. We should say we need 100 percent or 110 percent so that we actually get what we need if we want to be combat ready." • "Spend more of our $50 billion on unit-level resources. We are struggling on things like ink and paper."

Table 3.2—Continued

Theme	Description	Examples
Provide autonomy	Empower company leaders, support their authority, and trust them to do their jobs (i.e., "power down").	• "Allow more autonomy. Company and platoon leaders know their soldiers. I can't even schedule a range on my own."
Accelerate removal	Accelerate the time it takes for noncontributing soldiers to be removed from an active unit and/or the military.	• "Streamline the chapter process. MEB process is too slow and broken guys take up slots. Do it respectfully, but get them off the rolls." • "We need a lame duck company (for our med-board[b] guys)."
Follow schedules	Enforce predetermined agendas, timetables, and so on (e.g., from policy).	• "Maintain a consistent battle rhythm. Once that battle rhythm is established and if, for whatever reason, it cannot take place, instead of pushing it to later in the day/week, just cancel it."
Outsource	Contract civilians; leverage their specialized expertise and/or other available resources.	• "All the support stuff (gate guards, cutting grass, etc.) should be done by contractors. You lose soldiers not only to do the task but to train-up to do it. You could get so much more out of soldiers."

[a] Army Regulation 570-4 (*Manpower Management*, Washington, D.C.: Headquarters, Department of the Army, February 8, 2006) describes the term "borrowed military personnel" as the use of military personnel for special duties typically performed by government civilians or contracted services.

[b] "Med board" refers to an informal board of medical experts that evaluates the soldier's physical and/or mental condition to assess whether the soldier is fit to serve in full duty capacity.

MTOE = modified table of organization and equipment; BN = battalion; BDE = brigade; BOLC = Basic Officer Leader Course; DUI = driving under the influence; OJT = on-the-job training; COL = colonel; MEB = medical evaluation board.

Solutions Mentioned in Other Domains Are Similar

Prioritizing tasks was the most frequently mentioned time-management strategy we found mentioned outside the Army, followed by delegating tasks to subordinates, and then following schedules (see Table 3.3).

Table 3.3
Time-Management Solutions Common to All Domains

Theme	Examples
Prioritize	• "There really is no such thing as time management. . . . Instead, there's something called event control. And how do we control events? By planning and prioritizing. Simple advice, but . . . most people don't plan their days . . . because they claim they don't have the time. This, we're told, is like thinking that you can cut down a tree faster if you don't waste time sharpening your saw." [private sector literature][a] • "Think of focus as concentrated attention. Focused managers aren't in reactive mode; they choose not to respond immediately to every issue that comes their way or get sidetracked from their goals by distractions like email, meetings, setbacks, and unforeseen demands. Because they have a clear understanding of what they want to accomplish, they carefully weigh their options before selecting a course of action." [private sector literature]
Follow schedules	• "You can't eliminate interruptions, but you must minimize the number if you are going to work effectively. It takes time to warm up your mental motor after an interruption, so block your time— answer phone messages and email in blocks during the day. Don't destroy your concentration every time the message light comes on!"[b]

[a] Ed Brown. "Stephen Covey's New One-Day Seminar," *Fortune*, Vol. 139, No. 2, 1999, pp. 138–139.

[b] Gale Cutler, "Craig Takes Crash Course in Time Management," *Research-Technology Management*, Vol. 48, No. 6, 2005, pp. 57–60.

Other Domains Emphasize Organizing Information and "Pushing Back"

Although the time-management strategies we identified by analyzing non-Army sources were generally similar to those mentioned by our Army respondents, there were some potentially important differences in emphasis. Table 3.4 contains two uncommon themes in soldiers' responses: organizing information and "pushing back" on leader requests or taskings.

Organizing information was a commonly cited time-management approach in non-U.S. Army sources but was mentioned less by soldiers. This difference in approach may be attributed to soldiers lacking adequate administrative skills to think about how best to organize

Table 3.4
Time-Management Solutions Emphasized Less by Army Respondents Than by Other Sources

	Description	Examples
Organize information	Company commanders collect information (e.g., deadlines, requirements) and then "externalize" (i.e., write down) this information using tools such as checklists and calendars so that individuals can keep track of what is going on. This does not involve planning/prioritizing (i.e., making decisions about what should be accomplished)	• "Stay organized. To me, staying organized means finding a method to track everything that needs to be done."[a] • "What I'm learning, Allen says, is a process psychologists call 'distributed cognition'—getting all my nagging tasks, grand ideas, and unresolved projects out of my head and into his 'trusted system.' This will free my mind to think, dream, and focus on a single task rather than worrying about everything not getting done. 'Your mind is for having ideas,' Allen likes to say, 'not for holding them.'"[b]
Push back	Company leaders communicate with leaders at the BN level to appropriately negotiate what priorities exist for tasks directed by higher command, to include requesting the reconsideration of a decision, or to a "reclama."	• "Of all the time-management techniques ever developed, I've found that the most effective is the frequent use of the word no. You cannot protect your priorities unless you learn to decline—tactfully and firmly—every request that does not contribute to the achievement of your goals."[c]

[a] "Building Combat Ready Teams: The Crush of Requirements from Higher Headquarters," *Army*, Vol. 62, No. 8, August 2012, pp. 53–57.

[b] Paul Keegan, "Get a Life!" *Fortune*, Vol. 158, No. 4, September 1, 2008, pp. 114–120.

[c] Cutler, 2005.

NOTE: "Reclama" is a term commonly used in the military to request reconsideration of a decision or a change in policy.

and manage garrison duties. Our interviews at the brigade, battalion, and company level suggest gaps exist between what soldiers know and what they should know to perform many basic garrison duties. Part of the challenge might be attributed to a lack of experience on the job. By force structure design, company command tours last no more than two years, providing a relatively short period of time to gain depth in knowledge.

Programs and policies are often available to help soldiers and specifically company leaders navigate time-consuming activities such as personnel management, medical and legal processes, and other issues. For example, the Company Commander and First Sergeant Course programs of instruction include two days of training on the Command Supply Discipline Program (U.S. Army Inspector General Agency, 2012). Fort Hood's 1st Cavalry Division developed a garrison battle drills book covering recurring administrative tasks such as completing a unit commander's financial report, conducting inventories, and documenting disciplinary issues. The III Corps Troop School taught a Battalion Executive and S-3 Operations Officers Training Course that prepared them for key assignments. Fort Carson developed an at-risk soldier management tool to help commanders deal with health and wellness issues. While these types of courses can help soldiers navigate some administrative nuances, many of these courses are not offered Army-wide. Additionally, if available, the soldiers we interviewed were often either unaware of them, lacked the time to attend them, or felt that what was offered was inadequate to help them successfully execute company-level administrative responsibilities. Although project limitations precluded a deeper examination of such training courses, we can only speculate that this sense of inadequacy might be because these courses focus on specific tasks or issues and may not provide overarching strategies that can be applied across a spectrum of administrative taskings.

We identified several time-management principals in the literature that might apply to task management more broadly. At the individual level, setting goals and priorities, planning and scheduling, developing strategies for task completion, using mental simulations, and monitoring goal progress have been studied as ways to effectively use time (Häfner et al., 2014; Macan et al., 1990). Implementing quiet hours, which are scheduled periods of time when workers shut themselves out from external interruptions by closing their office doors or not answering phone calls, has garnered attention in the popular literature. One study has supported the effectiveness of this strategy, finding that using quiet hours for certain tasks helped increase performance on those tasks without additional work hours (König, Kleinmann, and Höhmann, 2013).

At the group or organizational level, Claessens et al. (2010) found levels of priority and urgency of tasks were associated with the completion of those tasks, suggesting that communicating the priority and urgency of certain tasks may be effective in increasing the likelihood of their completion. Studies have also examined the impact of the work environment, including supervisors, coworkers, and work processes, on the effectiveness of time-management strategies. Burt et al. (2010) labeled this the "time-management environment" and suggested positive personal interactions and efficient work processes facilitate productive time management.

"Pushing back" was a more commonly reported strategy from the interviews with nonmilitary leaders. However, some company leaders did address the issue of appropriately "pushing back" on taskings from their BN or above through one of two methods as follows:

- having built a relationship with the commander staff at BN level, engage in a discussion of the current taskings of the company (including documentation) and the new tasking with the goal of assessing the BN leadership's priorities
- using a formal process called "reclama" in which the commander requests the reconsideration of a decision made by echelons above.

Results from the focus groups suggested reclamas were done but seldom led to changes in taskings. However, some company leaders also described developing strong, trusted working relationships with members of their BN leadership. They reported being able to honestly communicate their documented taskings and concerns regarding lapses in the six-week lock-in requirement. Some have successfully managed to work with the BN leadership to rebalance taskings to ensure the leadership's needs were met and the company personnel were not overburdened.

Conclusion

The findings reported in this chapter highlight notable themes that emerged from our research. We found no silver bullet to eliminate the time-burden challenge. We did, however, develop some actionable recommendations that may help both higher headquarters and company leaders enable time-management best practices and avoid relying on counterproductive strategies. We present recommendations in the next chapter.

CHAPTER FOUR

Recommendations to Reduce Time Burdens

Synthesizing information from our multiple research methods, we identified what we consider some of the more feasible solutions based on current doctrine, discussions with focus groups and Army SMEs, and supporting evidence from the literature. We organized these solutions into three broad types of recommendations for company leaders and their supervisors to consider for reducing time burdens on company leaders as follows:

- mitigating job demands
- enhancing job resources
- facilitating changes to keep awareness of time burdens and improve the productive use of time.

Respectively, we label these categories *clarity, capital,* and *culture* (see Table 4.1). This categorization is based roughly on the JD-R model; clarity relates to job demands and capital relates to job resources. To elaborate, clarity pertains to practices aimed at reducing role conflict and work load, both of which contribute to job demands and have been found to be negatively related to burnout (Lee and Ashforth, 1996). Meanwhile, capital pertains to adding tangible resources that help commanders achieve their job or contribute to their development. Meta-analytic findings show increasing such job resources is associated with decrease in burnout and increase in job engagement (Crawford, LePine, and Rich, 2010; Lee and Ashforth, 1996). In addition, some strategies focus on changing the way people think about tasks, relationships, and policy at the organization level. Although this category

Table 4.1
Three Categories of Recommendations: Clarity, Capital, and Culture

Clarity	
Focused on mitigating job demands	
General recommendation	**Example**
• Define and concentrate effort on important tasks; critically screen urgent tasks	• Identify a limited number of priorities
• Timing matters: minimize distractions through consolidation and discipline	• Consolidate required trainings when permitted
• Know the time involved to complete taskings and focus on the meaning associated with metrics (red, amber, green)	• Determine complete time implications of taskings, including time effects on other activities
Capital	
Focused on improving job resources	
General recommendation	**Example**
• Augment access to, compatibility with, and capability of technical systems	• Replace DTMS
• Enhance formal training and support tools	• Improve teaching of administrative and managerial skills prior to promotion to leadership position
• Increase personnel available to company leaders to support administrative and installation support tasks	• Add Human Resource Specialists, Administrative System Digital Master Gunners[a] and/or DTMS clerks
Culture	
Focused on improving the job environment	
General recommendation	**Example**
• Enforce existing timeline-related doctrine and policy	• Enforce FORSCOM six-week lock-in policy
• Provide autonomy to company leaders	• Accept increased risk with new leaders to provide leader development opportunities
• Encourage pushback based on accurate assessment of current capabilities	• Reward honesty and highlight candor in Officer Evaluation Reports ratings

[a] An Administrative Systems Digital Master Gunner would be a subject matter expert who can configure, operate, maintain, and coordinate the connectivity of DTMS or other tracking systems of record. Creating such a position could ease company command staff's administrative burden so they can focus on core METL tasks.

pertains to providing resources, it intervenes at a deeper level closely tied to belief systems of military members and, at a larger scale, encompassing the entire military culture. Therefore, we kept this category separate and labeled it culture. Given the complex nature of the time-burden challenge facing company leaders, implementing any single solution is unlikely to yield much improvement. Substantial change will only come about through modifications on many fronts within each of these categories.

Within each recommendation category, we highlight three specific courses of action and discuss the feasibility of each one. These solutions are not novel: for example, our research indicates the U.S. Army already has policy that, if adhered to, would likely apply to many of our clarity and culture recommendations.

Some of our recommendations are actions for company leaders to take, and others require an organizational response from higher levels in the Army. At the organizational level, we sought to identify ways senior leadership might establish conditions that reduce or help manage the inordinate number of tasks not directly associated with company command core missions. At the individual level, we identified time-management strategies to help company leaders optimize the limited amount of time available to satisfy mission and training objectives.

Increase Clarity About Command Priorities and Resource Implications

We use the term "clarity" to refer to fostering unambiguous understanding and ongoing communication between relevant stakeholders with respect to (1) the primary role(s) and objective(s) for a given position, unit, and/or mission as well as (2) the ever-changing availability of resources and demands. Our research finds lack of clarity—described as role conflict and ambiguity—to be rampant among company leaders. In business literature, role conflict and ambiguity have long been recognized as contributing to negative outcomes for both the organization and the individual, including a higher likelihood of leaving, lower organizational commitment, and lower general satisfaction (Abramis, 1994; Fisher and Gitelson, 1983; Jackson and Schuler, 1985). Although prior research finds only weak negative relationships with performance, our research suggests role conflict and ambiguity are more strongly negatively related to performance in the context of an Army company, such as the satisfying effect associated with "just do it."

For the Army, a synthesis of our research suggests role conflict and ambiguity can be best reduced through three lines of effort: delineating what is important, minimizing distractions, and focusing on substantive issues.

Define and Concentrate Effort on Important Tasks; Critically Screen Urgent Tasks

We recommend both senior and company leaders take the time to identify and agree on a limited set of priorities that, while revisited to account for the ever-changing circumstances, remain constant and thus predictable. This senior leader's comment reinforces this recommendation:

> Strategic leaders must be deliberate and disciplined in their approach to using time, one of their most important assets. They must focus on the important, not just the urgent. A formal time-management system, not just a daily schedule, helps strategic leaders do that. Part of that formal system is a disciplined meeting rhythm, one that ensures that subordinates get all the guidance they need at the frequency they need it, thus creating time for thinking and "battlefield circulation"—both critical to strategic leaders. Establishing priorities, making time allocation to those priorities, synchronizing these allocations to the meeting rhythm and battlefield circulation program, and creating a method to evaluate the use of time are all critical to formal time-management strategies.

Likewise, company leaders should proactively seek out information on higher command priorities. The selection of what training to do often comes through discerning what training their commanders have emphasized. Similarly, one soldier advised delaying "knee-jerk" requirements that are suddenly prioritized by higher headquarters, stating "these tasks, though not trivial, are reactions to events elsewhere that are overprioritized." The commander should try to distinguish which ones are actually important and which can be delayed and will be forgotten about by higher headquarters, eliminating the need to complete them ("Building Combat Ready Teams: The Crush of Requirements from Higher Headquarters," 2012).

Once priorities are defined and shared, all other activities must be assessed to determine if they align with the stated priorities. Tasks not directly supporting such priorities should be discarded first. Activities detracting from the completion or efficient completion of the stated priorities ought to be scrutinized. Time and attention are limited and therefore must be used selectively.

Feasibility Check

Existing Army doctrine addresses some of the issues identified by company leaders with respect to leadership at the battalion level and higher in clarifying and prioritizing their objectives. The doctrine defining "Training Units and Developing Leaders" (ADP No. 7-0, 2016) specifies that prioritization is the role of the Senior Commander, typically at the division and brigade levels. This prioritization should then be published through the Commanders Training Guidance (CTG) (U.S. Department of the Army, 2016, p. 2-2, para. 2-6) via an annual memorandum. Further discussion between subordinate and senior commanders should occur during Quarterly Training Briefs based on the commander's Unit Training Plan that focuses on the specific tasks to train, which is based on the higher commander's guidance. Doctrine also specifies the role of "Commanders Dialogue"[1] (U.S. Department of the Army, 2016, chap. 1, para 1-71–1-73, Table 1-3) that provides guidance on the importance of discussions and dialogues between the unit and higher commander throughout the training process. These recurring dialogues help ensure both commanders agree with the direction and scope of unit.

---

[1] A satirical article on the "Duffle Blog" website (NotBenedictArnold, "Battalion Commander's List of Number One Priorities Hits 50," *Duffle Blog*, June 15, 2017) underscores the perspectives expressed by some company-level leaders who participated in our study.

Thus, we believe our recommendations fit within the bounds of current guidance and simply reinforce the need to effectively use pre-existing mechanisms to communicate and discern among urgent tasks. Implementing this existing doctrine to plan training and develop leaders will ensure more effective integration and prioritization of tasks at battalion and company levels.[2]

Timing Matters: Minimize Distractions Through Consolidation and Discipline

Over the course of our investigation we gained an increasing appreciation for timing. Timing refers to frequency, duration, and assignment of when and how tasks are accomplished. For example, although topics in AR 350-1 training are considered important, the timing of their execution can be frustrating due to their completion frequency or last-minute application. For example, one focus group participant described how the unit managed their time differently to accommodate training requirements:

> Not the elimination of programs, but a consolidation. SHARP, EO [equal opportunity], transgender: those can't go away. Everyone's got to do it, and I don't want to discount that it is important or it's not a problem, but I have units doing it weekly. The amount of AR 350-1 required weekly. In some cases [there are] daily touchpoints. There are times when I've agreed with the stand-down days. But you can whittle that down to 2–3 days. In Germany, we stood down for a week to do all the AR 350-1 requirements. Qualified on my weapons, took all my training. They had instructors at each different location, [and] you had a schedule based on section. The best time to do that is the summer PCS [permanent change of station] schedule. We're struggling to train anyways because we don't have anybody.

Grouping the execution of similar activities would help to reduce time transitioning between activities. Higher echelons of the Army and

---

2   eMILPO is the Army's Electronic Military Personnel Office system of records for tracking readiness for active-duty personnel.

company leaders could apply this principle to topics such as AR 350-1 training or medical readiness. Both the private and academic literature on time management noted the importance of dedicating blocks of time to certain activities (Brogan, 2010; König, Kleinmann, and Höhmann, 2013; Penttila, 2007; Pratt, 2000).

> I try to keep a routine such as a company meeting every Friday or check metrics every Monday. This routine keeps things on the radar; even if they are messed up, at least we have a plan.

Additionally, some researchers are starting to appreciate that not all times of the day are created equal and matching the task to the time of day may enhance effectiveness (Ariely and Wertenbroch, 2002; Pink, 2018). For example, an "early bird" might be more productive in the mornings and may want to take on more difficult tasks during the morning; in contrast, a "night owl" might prefer to wait until later in the afternoon to tackle more challenging taskings. Further, rearranging time schedules for certain unit activities might help soldiers save valuable working hours. One focus group participant suggested shifting a unit's physical training (PT) schedule from before work to afterward to eliminate the time needed to shower before coming to the office. These examples are illustrative and may not work for everyone (i.e., some may run into problems with childcare when work runs over, and others may not have time for PT at all). However, the approach offers a more nuanced way of thinking about how to organize activities to maximize productivity.

Finally, activities should be allotted just enough time to encourage their efficient use. For instance, meetings should be short and punctual and involve only essential personnel.

> One of [former Secretary of Defense Donald Rumsfeld's] best recommendations is "whatever the size or purpose of [the] meeting, start and end it on time." This may seem obvious, but too often in organizations the norm is for meetings to start late or run long. Leaders either tolerate it or worse, are the cause of it. Rumsfeld is able to demonstrate the actual harm this can cause. He uses an example to show how five hours of productive time

can be lost when a meeting starts 15 minutes late and there are 20 people present. Although 15 minutes does not seem like much in isolation, the cumulative act—five hours of lost productivity—can cause serious harm to an organization. Managing your organization's time through effectively run meetings is vital in today's military when we are facing budget crunches, and the new mantra is "do more with less."

Feasibility Check

Our recommendations are supported by evidence in the private sector literature. Specific examples, such as shifting the PT schedule to the afternoon, may not be feasible within a given garrison context. However, we judge the general philosophy, which aims to encourage flexibility in scheduling to allow units to tailor their time to optimize productivity, to be a sound approach.

Appreciate the Time a Tasking Requires and Focus on the Most Critical Metrics

Command decisions and associated requirements must be informed by an accurate understanding of the impact these requirements have on the personnel and other resources available to execute. Senior leadership should consider what information they must know about lower-level units and what information company leaders can retain for unit-level purposes. One senior-level individual we interviewed appreciated the increasing nature of information requirements on company leaders.

> Fourteen years ago, there were three things I had to tell my officer about; today there are 27 things I have to tell a brigade commander. Battery commanders have 27 different things.

Today's company leaders are expected to track significantly more information requirements.

> Readiness at that level should be viewed as an aggregate, not in the minutiae. The company and platoon commanders should know the minutiae, but the four-star doesn't need to know why this one guy is on medical. If I want to view something in aggre-

gate, the systems need to coordinate with each other. If the company commander hasn't put the APFT [Army Physical Fitness Test] in eMILPO13 and DTMS, they'll be viewed as lazy.

Focus group discussions also indicate higher-echelon leaders are substituting time-intensive PowerPoint briefing requirements for more personal participation in a unit's activities; they suggest more face time would help facilitate effective communication:

> If you want me to brief BN Co beforehand, why can't I come in and do it that way? I can take two hours to do that in person, face-to-face, a real mentoring and bonding session, or I can piss away 12 hours building a beautiful 30-slide PowerPoint presentation deck that makes you feel warm and fuzzy. That type of leadership doesn't happen when you're reading through confirmation briefs. That's a result of people feeling like they have too much to do to make a brief in person. Those are huge time sucks and breed resentment amongst men like me. If you give a shit about me, come out and give a shit about me. It doesn't show that you care when you ask me to make a presentation for you and email it to you and that's it. It's like telling me to make my own report card as a kid. It's not a test, and it doesn't give you a look at what I need.

Because increasing clarity involves reducing role conflict and ambiguity, senior leaders should clearly communicate what tasks are important and when are they important. Personal observations provide unique opportunities to understand subordinate perspectives, see the impact of requirements, and build relationships that can facilitate an effective negotiation of priorities. Junior leaders should actively think about how to allocate and optimize their time. Providing clearly thought-out and articulate explanations for how requirements impact a unit's status of readiness can help senior leaders better appreciate the challenges associated with meeting a given requirement. Both levels should contribute to a shared understanding of a unit's status and what must be done to succeed as well as agreement about where to accept risk.

Feasibility Check

Engaging directly with subordinates (but not inordinately so) will provide senior leaders with a better appreciation of the time impact taskings have on companies. This feasibility check is largely in line with existing doctrine laid out in *Field Manual 7-0* instructing commanders to engage in dialogue with subordinate units to ensure there is agreement on the direction and scope of unit training. Such engagement is intended to be used to seek information about the status of missions, needs, equipment, and soldiers (U.S. Department of the Army, 2016, chap. 1, para. 1-27–1-29). Doctrine also encourages both junior and senior commanders to engage in in-person dialogue and observations to gain a more holistic understanding of unit strengths and weaknesses (Army Doctrine Publication No. 7-0, 2018, para. 2-2). While doctrine supports a commitment to quality face time, discussions with junior and senior-level Army personnel suggest the current garrison operating environment makes it difficult to achieve as leaders at all levels struggle with competing taskings.

Provide Enhanced Capital Through Technology, Training, and Personnel

We use the term "capital" to refer to the tangible resources contributing to organizational functioning such as information systems, instructional programs, and personnel levels. Due to fiscal constraints and competing budgets, efforts to increase or enhance capital are undoubtedly difficult and often beyond the control of senior Army leadership. Nonetheless, even within the budgetary restrictions, more strategic consideration and investment must be devoted to the Army's technology, training, and personnel to reduce the time burdens on company leaders.

Augment Access to, Compatibility with, and Capability of Technical Systems

Technical systems meant to support company leaders can be clunky, redundant, unsynchronized, or otherwise insufficient. A lack of computer accessibility was singled out as an unrecognized waste of precious unit time. Limited computer accessibility appears to be a rather straightforward technology issue to address. The other information technology challenges require more complex resolutions. Specifically, many company leaders expressed the need for a single, comprehensive, user-friendly system to manage all their requirements:

> Combine all the electronic resources into a single, integrated environment.

> We have 14 or 15 databases that company commanders maintain: eMILPO, MEDPROS [Medical Protection System], commander's portal, G-Army, UCFR [Unit Commander's Financial Report], [and] about half of those at least don't talk to one another. If they want DTMS to work, you would have to have one system that has everything. Things consolidated and streamlined for the end user to communicate better, feed data to users—would cut down on man hours. Instead, we are submitting redundant information over and over and over, and then when you're almost finished with the report, the system crashes. Biggest chunk of time is tracking readiness.

Principles that should guide new technology development include simplicity, user-friendliness, compatibility with other systems, and consideration about how the increased data will be used within the force structure and decisionmaking process (Burke, 2017).

Compatibility is key, but DoD often struggles to develop fully compatible systems.[3] That is bad news for company leaders, who often need to cross-reference multiple Army databases—one for supply, one for personnel, another for training—to answer basic questions. To the greatest extent possible, DoD should embrace open-source software—the same technology that allows rival software companies to easily

---

[3] For example, according to a 2018 GAO report, "DOD officials stated that there are over 800 fragmented information technology systems used to store and record training records across the department" (U.S. GAO, *Defense Management: DOD Needs to Address Inefficiencies and Implement Reform Across Its Defense Agencies and DOD Field Activities*, Washington, D.C.: U.S. GAO, GAO-18-592, September 2018).

share information across platforms. Compatible technology was a key theme emerging from focus group discussions:

> Keep it simple. A simple smartphone app allows me to sort through a database of every beer I've consumed in the past five years, export it to an Excel spreadsheet, and sort my libations in too many ways. The best four-star-rated stout brewed in Oregon I sampled in 2013? I can find it in seconds. But sorting through military databases to find the right information isn't quite so easy. Usability should be a key criterion when developing Army software. In a perfect world, leaders would be able to get the information they need without relying on staffs or subordinates.

> We have too many systems in the Army right now, [and] they are not linked together. The only two linked systems are the email and NetUSR; DTMS doesn't see that. Higher up at the BN level, we ask is that unit ready to go to war? If that's the case, we should ask are these things linked together? At the company level, it should be a one-stop shop. We make them build the base of the pyramid. The CO should only have to put something into one system, and it should go up from there. Right now it's reversed.

The DTMS was the most cited technology tool hampering productivity:

> We need a hub. There are so many different websites—e.g., DTMS—[and] none of the training automatically feeds. It's ridiculous that our systems don't talk [to each other]. Have to print off a certificate and then take it to the DTMS operators. We are not authorized operators to run the systems, so it's an additional task that we have to peg someone to do.

> If you got rid of DTMS there would be a lot of time saved. There would be less documentation lost by mailing through USPS than using this system. The Army is so hell-bent on going digital, but nothing is based on off-the-shelf; everything is proprietary.

> It's completely inefficient to deal with DTMS; wastes countless man hours.

Figure 4.1
The Process to Record APFT Scores in DTMS

A related challenge pertains to the purgatory between digital and analog. In Figure 4.1, we outline the process one company follows to maintain its DTMS as well as two backups: a paper tracker and supplementary digital tracker (in Excel). This company dedicated one soldier full-time to ensuring the DTMS system and backups are up to date. The "DTMS operator" image below hung over the DTMS operator's work station in one company's training room.

In addition to investing in software technology advancements, one officer's suggestion for designing such integrated systems was to invite software developers to shadow companies to gain an appreciation of their needs. Another was to provide company leaders opportunities to intern or otherwise engage with IT developers to help inform system requirements for efficiently meeting their needs.

Feasibility Check

The limits of our research precluded a deeper investigation into the technology acquisitions process to understand the potential challenges associated with investments in new software. We suspect the costs, certain contractual barriers, and lead time to employment would be significant. However, establishing information-sharing opportunities along the lines of personnel exchanges appears to be a relatively quick, cost-effective professional development-enhancing approach worth considering.

Enhance Formal Training and Support Tools

As we discussed above, consolidation of required trainings is one promising approach to improving time management. A second training-related approach is improving the courses provided prior to taking a leadership position, both general courses conducted by the Army[4] and the garrison-specific pre-command course, which is intended to familiarize company commanders with resources at a specific installation before they take command. One recommendation from a post command captain was to have the different garrison agencies explain the process of their interaction with company command teams using recent trends during the pre-command course. He said many agencies simply introduced themselves and handed out their contact information. If these officers and NCOs are taken from their units for two weeks, there is potential to increase their knowledge of "how to" act as a command team during the pre-command course. Although a training evaluation was beyond the scope of this study, we heard a range of perspectives suggesting variability and possible gaps:

> I think having different agencies around post with a 30-minute block come talk with a face and a name with a touchpoint. Like if someone were to enroll in ASAP [Army Substance Abuse Program]. Who is it that they're going to? Having them in a central location was beneficial.

> Formal training—as far as being taught how to be a commander, there is a pre-command course, but I haven't been to it. So maybe that is part of the problem.

> "BOLC [Basic Officer Leader Course] taught me to be an engineer but not a leader. Train us [in] ways to manage people and talk with soldiers; what do you say when they have ended their career with a DUI [driving under the influence]? Handling things at the personal level is all OJT."

---

[4]   Examples include Basic Officer Leader Course, Captains Career Course, Warrior Leader Course, Advanced Leader Course, and Senior Leader Course.

An initial review of the Maneuver Captains Career Course Program of Instruction (POI) suggests there may be potential for including administrative and managerial skills. The POI does expose the captains to family readiness programs, military justice, unit maintenance, and elective command topics by BCT type. It does not, however, dedicate a significant portion of time to these topics. Also, these topics are condensed into the last module. Perhaps these topics could be spread out and allocated more time throughout the course, increasing overall "time-on-task" and providing "spaced" versus "massed" training on these skills. There is evidence that spacing the training out, over time, can provide improved understanding learning and retention (Donovan and Radosevich, 1999).

In addition to improved training, there is an opportunity to develop shared documentation capturing useful information about company leader activities, including time-management approaches, in a succinct manner. This material may be especially useful for leaders early in their leadership role:

> During my first command, I felt like I was drowning in the tidal wave of on-the-job training that comes in the wake of things like congressional letters, DUIs, testing hot on a urinalysis, arrests, suicide ideation, etc. By my second command, I had a smartbook with all the regulations, policies and action-step checklists, which allowed me to be much more efficient and effective. I recommend building a book like that before you take command. A great place to start is the Commander's and First Sergeant's Quick Reference Guide to Army Regulations. Both the guide and my own battle rhythm are posted in the company commander forum.

Such documentation can take various forms. For example, the U.S. Marine Corps utilizes "turnover folders," which

> include information about policy, personnel, status of pending projects, references, management controls, functioning of the section, ways and means of accomplishing routine as well as infrequent tasks, and other information of value to an individual assigned to that billet. The Major subordinate command Main-

tenance Management Standard Operating Procedures must state the requirement, contents, details, and the billets that require turnover folders.[5]

A recent application in the Army adopts a "common events" approach, which provides leaders generic outlines with information specific to the situations for how to handle common occurrences.

The use of checklists to support process and decisionmaking accuracy has been championed by the aircraft industry for decades and has come into prominence in the business and medical professions (Gawande, 2009). Gawande cites the use of checklists across many domains to provide "greater efficiency, consistency and safety." The use of checklists and "smartbooks" in emergency response are growing. The National Incident Management System was implemented to aid in the effectiveness of responses to large-scale emergencies following the September 11, 2001, terrorist attacks. The organizational structure and processes are roughly based on operations center models in the U.S. military and are foreign to most nonmilitary personnel involved in emergency responses. So, like for many complex, enterprise-scale operations, there is a pocket "field guide" for people involved to support the transition to and execution of the operation (Ward, 2007). A photo of the guide, printed on waterproof paper, and its sections are presented in Figure 4.2. Similar pocket guides exist for other federal, medical, fire, and police organizations, processes, and activities.

Providing quick access to procedures to help deal with common events confronted by new company leaders could be implemented locally at a brigade, division, or corps. This initiative could start by simply having a BN staff member who has completed company command in the BN (perhaps before next assignment) record the standard operating procedures (SOPs) at that post to handle specific situations such as Legal, SHARP/EO, Serious Incident Reports, Chapter Process, and training calendar. The document would include specific

---

[5] "The Marine Corps Integrated Maintenance Management System (MIMMS) is a set of manual procedures by which the effective use of personnel, money, facilities, and materiel as applied to the maintenance of ground equipment is controlled" (MCO P4790.2C, *MIMMS Field Procedures Manual*, Washington, D.C.: Headquarters, U.S. Marine Corps, 2013).

Figure 4.2
Example of a Pocket "Field Guide" or "Smartbook" for Responders to Large-Scale Incidents

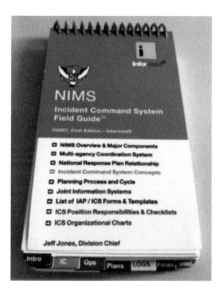

NOTE: Such a guide could benefit company leaders, especially early in their command.

names and contact information for key stakeholders in each process. Although it would take substantial effort to establish the first version, subsequent iterations would only involve updates. The document could be inspected by a brigade commander during every company change of command out brief. While this requirement would take place at lower echelons of command, the practice should be institutionalized to ensure it occurs Army-wide for consistency.

Increase Personnel Available to Company Leaders to Support Administrative and Installation Support Tasks

The role of the company leader is to command soldiers preparing for their unit's mission set. In the current operating environment, however, company leaders and their units are increasingly distracted with responsibilities involving more administrative and support tasks. Although soldiers consider delegation a top strategy to reduce the burdens, they also expressed frustration about not having the requisite numbers of trained and designated personnel to delegate to: "Manning is what is killing us." We recommend ancillary tasks be assigned to newly created positions both internal and external to the Army. Company leaders (and soldiers) should focus on only what they as leaders can do and should have enough personnel to whom they can delegate tasks others can do effectively. Specifically, we suggest the Army authorize administration positions, outsource installation support taskings, and accelerate the time it takes for noncontributing soldiers to be removed from an active unit and/or the military.

The authorization of internal administration positions is largely a formal recognition of and improvement over what already occurs. Currently, company leaders must assign soldiers who are frequently untrained and/or unmotivated to perform administrative functions to support the many responsibilities associated with the collection, examination, and reporting of unit readiness data. Given the emphasis on readiness tracking, we recommend the Army consider authorizing an Modification Table of Organization and Equipment (MTOE) position specifically dedicated to unit administrative tasks (and protected from outside taskings). Several examples emerged in our discussions: 42A Human Resource Specialists, Administrative Systems Digital Master Gunners, and DTMS clerks. The 42As would focus on the broader human resources issues, and the Administrative Systems Digital Master Gunners would devote their attention to unit-training-specific topics with assistance from the DTMS clerk. To incentivize these roles, their promotional potential will need to be considered (e.g., create an additional skill identifier to recognize the formal training and completion of these skills).

Feasibility Check

Changes to a POI at any Army training organization are difficult: Instructors and staff will attest to the very limited number of contact hours they get with their trainees and the large amount of curriculum material to be covered. Increasing the time spent on teaching personnel management skills during any of the leadership development courses would require topics to be shortened or dropped and reportedly is unlikely to be implemented. However, spacing such training out in a POI would not add time to the overall total but would provide the potential benefits of interspersing instruction among other elements of learning. One can imagine the amount of discussion over the course of the training if there were compelling personnel management "case studies" with lessons learned distributed throughout a course versus having a single section during the course.

The process of developing, producing, and testing the effectiveness of "Common Events Approaches" handbooks or "rich checklists" for Army SOPs was done as part of an Army lieutenant colonel's dissertation on knowledge management (Gayton, 2009). During an evaluation of the concept, small spiral-bound sets of "Common Events" cards were produced summarizing the experiences of 330 Stryker Brigade Combat Team combat returnees. These "cargo pocket" publications were provided to some soldiers from two Stryker Brigade Combat Teams during their combat training center rotation prior to deploying to combat operations in Iraq. SOPs were for common events in what would be their area of operations and included events such as "(P)IED— identified by patrol," "Quick Reaction Force (QRF)—respond as QRF to 'hot' areas," and "Dismounted patrol takes sniper/small arms fire." Each common event had three sets of checklists: "Common actions/ reminders," "Equipment/kits/tools to support operations," and "Event execution checklist." Having such support tools for new company leaders could potentially provide faster, more accurate, and less risky responses to common events faced by company leaders, especially early in their commands. Increasing administrative support through adding an administrative specialist to each company would require significant changes to force structure and finding personnel to fill such slots that are reportedly beyond the resources of the current Army.

We also suggest evaluating the time savings and potential quality improvements in property accountability that might be gained from outsourcing this administrative task. As illustrated in Figures 2.3 and 2.4 in Chapter Two, company leaders spend roughly 18 percent of their time on duties associated with accountability and maintenance. Prior RAND research benchmarking Army property accountability practices against other branches of the U.S. military, government, and commercial organizations found the U.S. Navy used civilians to carry out property accountability activities.[6]

Outsourcing and/or expanding installation support taskings is likely to alleviate much frustration and provide more opportunities for soldiers to perform their core tasks, facilitating skill development and retention.[7] For example, one respondent stated, "soldiers don't think that they are soldiers anymore. We are gardeners. It's crazy." These installation support roles would include responsibilities currently associated with borrowed military manpower (BMM) (e.g., air assault school instructors, liaisons) and regularly occurring garrison support tasks (e.g., gate guard, grass cutting, card reading). Many leaders who could be supporting their company are away from their units for extended periods while executing duties to meet someone else's priorities. Also, company leaders find themselves and their soldiers spending a significant amount of their time planning and executing garrison support rather than conducting the prerequisite training to execute their mission-essential tasks:

> Allocate money to hire people to do the BMM tasks—civilian instructors, guards. Get BMM out of units who are trying to train including SHARP and EO so the company commander would have more people.

> We need more agencies. If I don't have the resources, then I can't solve it. Mental health, behavioral health and physicals—I have to chapter this guy, and it's a 2–3-week wait for every appointment.[8]

Outsourcing installation support taskings is an issue of financial resource and contracting capabilities. While the limits of this study

---

[6]   Caitlin Hawkins et al., unpublished RAND Corporation research, 2010.

[7]   Lytell et al. found similar challenges for Army Intelligence Analysts. This study found junior and midgrade analysts spent approximately 70 percent of their time performing non-military intelligence tasks, which hinders retention of perishable skills acquired during initial training. See Maria C. Lytell et al., *Assessing Competencies and Proficiency of Army Intelligence Analysts Across the Career Life Cycle*, Santa Monica, Calif.: RAND Corporation, RR-1851-A, 2017.

[8]   The term "chapter out" refers to the specific Army regulation describing the type of reason for a discharge.

preclude a deeper dive into potential barriers, investing in additional manpower merits further consideration.

Soldiers who are not contributing to the unit's effectiveness and are unlikely to do so in the near future should be removed quickly from the company-level roster and, if appropriate, from the Army.

> Dealing with high-risk soldiers takes a lot of time. Your deployability is determined by how many are deployable, and the guys that hurt you are those (1) med-boarding (medical evaluation) and (2) going through an administrative chapter. Those two numbers are nondeployables, and they hurt your readiness and you have to spend time constantly applying pressure to make sure that they are sped along. It requires constant attention and pressure. It is about talking to Soldier for Life medical providers. You are fighting against other commanders.

One option we considered would be for nondeployable individuals with nonmedical-related issues to be consolidated into a single unit and their needs addressed accordingly. The Army might explore establishing a battalion-level unit similar in construct to the Warrior Transition Unit (WTU).[9] The unit would focus on soldiers who require administratively intensive support for legal issues or other matters not covered in a WTU. The unit would be located at the battalion level, and leadership would be rotated among battalions. This approach would shift the responsibility of the noncontributing soldier away from company leaders and free up a valuable position in an extremely limited roster.

Feasibility Check

On July 30, 2018, the Army enacted guidance instructing that service members who are considered nondeployable for more than 12 consecutive months are subject to evaluation for retention (DoD Instruction 1332.45, 2018). We discussed this policy change with Army SMEs who felt not only that speeding up the process for discharging nondeployable soldiers would be the best approach but also that a separate unit

---

[9] The Warrior Transition Unit program is available at installations across the Army and focuses on providing support to wounded soldiers who require a minimum of six months of rehabilitative care, therapy, or complex medical management.

could serve as a viable stop gap measure. Due to the potential downfalls with respect to morale and possible stigmatization, we suggest ensuring the unit is staffed with individuals with specific expertise to address these issues with the assumption that there are others better qualified than company commanders to provide such professional support.

Reinforce a Culture that Builds Trust and Encourages Candor and Autonomy

Culture is deep rooted and permeates all aspects of organizational life.[10] For any new time-management approaches to succeed in the Army, they must be anchored in a culture that builds trust and empowers company leaders to apply disciplined initiative to determine how to prioritize and perform non–mission-essential job tasks. These concepts fit within the core tenets of mission command (ADP No. 6-0, 2012) yet appear easier to establish in doctrine than to execute in practice. But there are tangible ways senior leaders can demonstrate their commitment to reducing the time burden on their company leaders. To start, senior leadership must establish a command climate that (1) enforces policies designed to protect company leaders' time; (2) provides company leaders autonomy to manage their own and their unit's time; (3) encourages pushback on unrealistic time demands when appropriate; and (4) rewards honesty, when warranted, about what is feasible.

Enforce Existing Timeline-Related Doctrine and Policy

Many extant Army policies are intended to standardize appropriate timelines, such as the six-week locked-in training schedule freeing companies from short notice taskings. FORSCOM's FY 18 training guidance reinforced the lock-in policy, as described in *Field Manual 7-0*, noting every echelon's responsibility to ensure company leaders are

---

[10] Meredith et al. identify several mutually reinforcing elements driving cultural change to include goals, accountability, training, resources, and engagement. In this respect, senior Army leadership must establish an overarching environment that facilitates change at lower levels. See Lisa S. Meredith et al., *Identifying Promising Approaches to U.S. Army Institutional Change*, Santa Monica, Calif.: RAND Corporation, RR-1588-A, 2017.

afforded a reasonable level of predictability to effectively plan, manage, and execute their mission training:

> We all have a role to play in this endeavor. One effective way to protect subordinates' time is to instill tasking discipline. I take my responsibilities very seriously in adhering to tasking policy in my headquarters, and I ask that you do the same at your level. Our best unit leaders personally analyze and make decisions on time management early and often enough to enable long-range planning, mitigate risk, and, ultimately, achieve sustained readiness. (U.S. Army Forces Command, 2017)

The "one-third–two-thirds rule"[11] also aims to strike a fair balance between meeting higher headquarter requirements and reserving adequate time for company commanders to command. As one senior military officer we consulted explained,[12]

> The 1/3s–2/3s rule works this way . . . one-third at each level. If a task has to occur in 90-hours:
>
> - Division = 30 of 90-hours (very complex organization and greater synchronization of resources is required)
> - BCT = 20 of 60-hours (less complex planning)
> - Battalion = 13 of 40-hours
> - Company = 9 of 27 hours
> - Platoon = 18-hours (very simple planning and little synchronization required).

Establishing policy is not enough, however. Company leaders doubted the Army's commitment to enforcing them.

> It's supposed to be one third to staff it and two thirds to execute it. It's not happening. We just got a tasking for a salute, and we

---

[11] This is meant to be a "guide to allocate time available. They use one-third of the time available before execution for their planning and allocate the remaining two-thirds of the time available before execution to their subordinates for planning and preparation" (U.S. Department of the Army, *Field Manual 5-0: The Operations Process*, Washington, D.C.: U.S. Army, 2010).

[12] Comments from senior military official, April 9, 2019.

found out yesterday. We got a call last Tuesday. We have to be in a parade in 30 minutes.

It's a joke. Show me the brigade core policy. Their reaction would be that you aren't a team player. The other side of this, though, they hold company commanders to this policy. If you wanted to get an M-4 range training next week, you would have to jump through so many hoops. Brigades and battalions are not held accountable, and company level is held accountable.

The challenge is one of "portion control." Higher headquarters must recognize the impact of their collective taskings on a unit's calendar and uphold their commitment to protect and respect company leaders' time. At the same time, leadership at every level must be held accountable for complying with the policies and practices being implemented to lessen time-burden problems.

Provide Autonomy to Company Leaders

Senior leaders should empower company leaders and trust them to do their jobs with discretion and independence. This is a key tenet of mission command (ADP No. 6-0, 2012). Autonomy enables effective time management because it provides individuals who likely have a better understanding of the local work environment with the authority to leverage existing opportunities and allocate constrained resources (Maylett, 2016). Senior leaders must assume risk and trust that their subordinates will demonstrate the professional judgment required to effectively carry out their commander's intent. As relatively new leaders, this judgment may not always be right, but autonomy is needed to provide opportunities for learning and development. Inexperienced leaders can learn as much—if not more—from failures as they can from successes (Trimailo, 2017). Give them the space to stumble, fall, and pick themselves up from minor missteps in garrison. This approach builds critical thinking skills necessary for the type of quick and decisive decisionmaking required when it counts most: on the battlefield. As one critic noted,

Expecting audacity among junior leaders in combat while micromanaging them in peacetime garrisons is a recipe for battlefield failure. The Army must restore its commitment to decentralized leadership and frontline leaders' authority, and practice what it preaches in garrison as well during operations. (Barno and Bensahel, 2016)

On the surface, there seems an inherent tension between finding ways to provide predictability and stability along the lines of what this study recommends and encouraging the type of audacity and flexibility required for battlefield performance. However, it is our belief the former actually supports the latter.[13] As one focus group participant opined,

Disciplined initiative is what drives things in the Army, and you can't really have that without autonomy. But autonomy requires trust, and that takes more time than we get/have.

Encourage Pushback, Based on an Accurate Assessment of Current Capabilities, and Reward Honesty

In a 2016 speech, Chief of Staff of the Army General Mark Milley shared his vision of the type of soldiers needed to win future wars. These soldiers may be operating in contested environments with enemies capable of cutting off communication between higher headquarters and subordinate units, General Milley noted, and characterized tomorrow's soldiers as comfortable operating without supervision, possessing acumen and the

willingness to disobey specific orders to achieve the intended purpose, the willingness to take risks to meet the intent, the accep-

---

[13] Organization theory suggests that innovative culture and disciplined, hierarchical structure can exist simultaneously, even symbiotically, within one organization. See Craig Whittinghill, David Berkowitz, and Phillip A. Farrington, "Does Your Culture Encourage Innovation?" *Defense Acquisition Research Journal*, Vol. 22, No. 2, April 2015, pp. 216–239; C. Gresov, "Designing Organizations to Innovate and Implement: Using Two Dilemmas to Create a Solution," *Columbia Journal of World Business*, Vol. 19, No. 4, 1984, pp. 63–67; and Ulla Eriksson-Zetterquist, Tomas Müllern, and Alexander Styhre, *Organization Theory: A Practice Based Approach*, Oxford, U.K.: Oxford University Press, 2011.

tance of failure and practice in order to learn from experimentation: these are all going to have to be elevated in the pantheon of leader traits. (Lopez, 2016, emphasis added)

In support of this vision, Army leaders must find ways to encourage and protect open debate and to legitimate (while tactful) disagreement when garrison tasks consume more time than companies have to complete them. This form of "selective disobedience" can be implemented if senior leaders take the time to engage with their company commanders to ensure only those who have proven to be responsible custodians of unit time can respectfully decline a tasking.

This concept is not wholly new. As General Robert Shoemaker once remarked, "You will impress me if I come to your training site and you tell me what parts of my guidance you have chosen not to follow. You will really impress me if you have already told my staff and explained why" (Burke, 2016). We identified instances where soldiers appear to have embraced this philosophy, as one company commander described in an online forum:

So I just stopped answering. I deleted emails that had been thoughtlessly forwarded with "HOT" and walked away from a ringing phone if I was on the way out to troop the line. That probably sounds childish, but it was intentional and thought out. That was the only way I could force those on the other end (staff mostly) to think farther ahead and not rely on the assumption that I would jump through hoops to make their urgent deadline. It caused some friction at first, but the volume of calls and emails decreased to only the ones that were actually HOT. When I had the inevitable confrontation with a staff officer all full of piss and vinegar who tracked me down on the flight line to find out why I had blown off the last "10 reports," I just shrugged my shoulders and said, "Well, sir, I was busy commanding." ("Building Combat Ready Teams: The Crush of Requirements from Higher Headquarters," 2012)

While we heard similar stories among focus group participants, they were rare. Within the context of a downsizing military, few company leaders interviewed felt they could reclama for fear that honestly reporting difficulties with accomplishing a tasker would reflect negatively on their professional careers. Interestingly, from the battalion-level perspective, interviews and discussions with O-4 level officers suggest such apprehension is largely self-inflicted. On more than one occasion we heard that when junior leaders kept their training schedule up to date and were able to document and articulate the conflict to higher echelons, together, they were usually able to resolve the problem of competing taskings without a negative impact on a junior leader's job, much less his or her career.

Of course, this negotiation is a two-way street. Higher echelons need to be receptive to this kind of selective disobedience and can demonstrate this by rewarding rather than punishing junior leaders for engaging in frank dialogue. A thoughtfully worded Officer Evaluation Report (OER) may provide an opportunity for senior leadership to reinforce the importance and value placed on developing effective time-management skills, including when they selectively disobey a tasking for appropriate reasons.[14]

At the same time, senior leaders should also be acknowledged for supporting effective time-management strategies. The Multi-Source Assessment and Feedback Program, which allowed junior leaders to weigh in on commanders' performances, would have provided an opportunity for junior leaders to highlight a supervisor's commitment. However, the program was among a series of requirements recently eliminated in a Headquarters, Department of the Army effort to reduce time-consuming activities that soldiers might otherwise spend

---

[14] We asked BN-level officers how rater comments noting a soldier's candor would be received. There was some qualified hesitation. As one O-4 level SME explained, "Commanders and promotion boards want to see evaluations that reflect potential and outstanding performance. If the comments in the OER reflect someone that is trying to 'go against the grain, but is honest,' probably not the message to send. Rather comments in the OER should reflect the hardships that the individual faced with reporting readiness, and what steps and procedures they implemented to get positive results." Additionally, Congress recently passed a significant reform to the military officers' promotion system that encourages a more merit-based decisionmaking process. The aim is to emphasize performance rather than seniority and could provide room for more nuanced evaluations, such as including how individuals manage their time. See Leo Shane III, "Congress Is Giving the Officer Promotion System a Massive Overhaul," *Military Times*, July 25, 2018.

building and sustaining combat readiness (Army Directive 2018-07-8, 2018). Another mechanism might be the command climate survey, which seeks to capture perceived attitudes and behaviors affecting morale within a given command. Company leaders could use this forum to spotlight actions taken by senior leaders demonstrating their commitment to promoting productive time use practices.

In many respects, the feasibility of our recommendations rests on the Army's commitment to uphold and enforce its current doctrine. There are mechanisms already in place to alleviate many of the burdens competing for company leaders' time. However, many individuals we spoke with were skeptical that Army culture is ready to make sincere adjustments. Culture change doesn't happen overnight, but our recommendations offer tangible strategies both senior leadership and company leaders can employ to shift further toward a more balanced and time-effective garrison environment. Senior leadership can start by trusting their subordinate leaders to meet commanders' intent; rewarding critical thinking, even when it leads to respectful resistance; providing guidance more than punishment when they fail; enforcing a degree of predictability; and protecting company commanders from external disruptions that are preventing them from achieving critical mission objectives. It is difficult to manage time that is not truly your own. If company leaders are encouraged to think critically; are provided enough authority to plan and execute commander's intent; are trusted to make the right decisions; and are provided a safe environment to fail, learn, and grow, they can feel emboldened to manage their time and use it wisely.

CHAPTER FIVE

Conclusions

The Army's company leaders have a lot on their plates. Our survey revealed they are willing to work long hours to meet DoD and Army requirements and accomplish higher headquarter taskings but would welcome some relief. Company leaders, on average, work 12.5-hour days in garrison, which takes a toll on their personal and family lives and may affect their ability to excel and advance in their professional careers as officers. Many company leaders we engaged with expressed frustrations about the high demands and the sometimes inadequate level or type of resources to meet those demands. On average, they estimated their workdays would need to be two hours shorter—ten hours long rather than 12—to maintain a healthy balance between work and other life demands. Even with such a reduction, company leaders would still be among the hardest-working Americans. However, given the number, variety, and importance of the tasks involved in their jobs, reducing their time burdens will not be easy or straightforward.

Of course, the problem of too much to do and too little time to do it is not confined to the Army. We searched widely for effective solutions to the time-burden problem in online Army literature (RallyPoint, *Small Wars Journal*, U.S. Naval Institute Blog, and War on the Rocks), academic databases (PsycArticles, PsycINFO, and Web of Science), and popular management literature (*Entrepreneur*, *Forbes*, *Fortune*, and *Inc.*). We uncovered a large number of solutions—some implemented and proven, some only proposed. By and large, they were similar to time-management strategies mentioned by our Army respondents, though they did not always receive the same emphasis in the Army as in other work domains. Although we did not discover any time-management strategies previously unknown to the Army, we identified specific ways to apply them in the context of company leadership in the Army. These are summarized in Table 5.1.

Some recommendations are organizational level and have significant resource implications. For example, increasing personnel responsible for administrative tasks or installation support will require additional manpower along with the associated costs. Others, such as keeping meetings brief and the list of attendees short, require only thoughtful consideration and respect for the time company leaders must devote to them. Company command-level leaders also have an important role to play in managing available time. They must proactively seek out guidance, training opportunities, and other support to help them effectively navigate the garrison working environment. As with any profession, effective time management comes with experience in the job, but that experience can be enhanced by careful implementation of a wide range of strategies meant to reduce the time burden.

There is no quick fix to the time-burden problem. To substantially reduce the time burden on company leaders, we conclude the Army will need to implement a variety of time-management strategies concurrently, systematically, and consistently. The Army's senior leadership has already laid the foundation for reducing the time burden through doctrine, policies, and Army studies devoted to the problem. One of the biggest challenges appears to be implementing them in practice. Using our menu of time-management recommendations, the Army should develop a sustained, multipronged attack on the time-burden problem. Though progress will be gradual, through a concerted effort, the Army can successfully reduce the time burdens of company commanders so their work days are long but not excessively so.

Many of the recommendations require a change in the culture or deep-rooted systems within the Army. Because the Army, as a functional hierarchical system, focuses on command training guidance to execute any given mission, these changes will only occur if leaders at all levels make alleviating the demands at the company level a priority. These recommendations will take focus and time. If made a priority, company leaders throughout the Army will benefit.

Table 5.1
High-Level Recommendations to Reduce Time Burdens on Company Leaders

	BURDEN	RECOMMENDATION		IMPLEMENTATION RESPONSIBILITY	
	Description	General	Example	Lead	Support
CLARITY Focused on mitigating job demands	Overtasking by higher echelons	1. Define and concentrate effort on important tasks; critically screen urgent tasks	Identify a limited number of priorities	ACOM/ASCCs/ DRUs	Corps thru Battalion CDRs
	Competing taskings from multiple higher echelons	2. Timing matters: minimize distractions through consolidation and discipline	Consolidate mandatory training when permitted	ACOM/ASCCs/ DRUs	Corps thru Battalion CDRs
	Lack of senior leadership's understanding of time requirements	3. Appreciate tasking time	Determine complete time implications of taskings, including time effects on other activities	ACOM/ASCCs/ DRUs	Corps thru Company leaders
	Hyperfocus on details rather than substance	4. Focus on metric meaning	Make the readiness of a unit a priority, not the readiness metrics	ACOM/ASCCs/ DRUs	Corps thru Battalion CDRs

Table 5.1—Continued

BURDEN	RECOMMENDATION		IMPLEMENTATION RESPONSIBILITY	
Description	General	Example	Lead	Support
CAPITAL — Focused on improving job resources				
Lack of resources at the company level	5. Augment access to, compatibility with, and capability of technical systems	Replace or improve DTMS	TRADOC	Training Management Directorate
Lack of skills/experience at the company level	6. Enhance formal training and support tools	Improve teaching of administrative and managerial skills prior to leadership position	ACOM/ASCC/ DRUs and TRADOC (CCC)	Corps thru Batallion CDRs
Lack of personnel at the company level	7. Increase personnel available to company leaders to support administrative and installation support tasks	Add Human Resource Specialists, Administrative System Digital Master Gunners, and/or DTMS clerks	TRADOC Centers of Excellence	HQDA (G1 and G3), HRC and FORSCOM (G3 Training)
CULTURE — Focused on improving the job environment				
Lack of commitment to reducing the time burden	8. Enforce existing timeline-related doctrine and policy	Enforce Forces Command six-week lock-in policy	ACOM/ASCCs/ DRUs	Corps thru BattalionCDRs
Unwillingness to accept prudent risk	9. Provide autonomy to company leaders	Accept increased risk with new leaders to provide leader development opportunities	Brigade CDRs	Battalion CDRs
Reluctance by company commanders to report honestly	10. Encourage pushback, based on accurate assessment of current capabilities	Reward honesty and highlight candor in Officer Evaluation Reports ratings	Brigade CDRs	Battalion CDRs Company leaders

NOTE: ACOM = Army Commands; ASCC = Army Service Component Command; CCC = Captain's Career Course; CDR = commander; DRU = direct reporting unit; DTMS = Digital Training Management System; FORSCOM = U.S. Army Forces Command; HQDA = Headquarters, Department of the Army; HRC = Human Resources Command; and TRADOC = Training and Doctrine Command.

Potential Future Research

The time-burden challenge is not new and is unlikely to go away soon. It is also not limited to the issues explored in this report. For example, company commanders have more than just excessive job demands with which to contend. Presumably, other factors such as family obligations or health conditions can add to the list of responsibilities for junior leaders. Similarly, soldiers' experiences prior to joining the Army likely influence how they cope with and prepare for a life of service. While beyond the scope of this report, further research providing a more holistic picture of the life of a young soldier could provide useful insights into how to facilitate professional development and achieve a successful, rewarding career in the Army.

Survey Administered During Focus Groups

DO NOT PUT YOUR NAME ON THIS HANDOUT
PLEASE SPELL OUT ALL ACRONYMS

SECTION A: Background Questions

1. What is your MOS (e.g., 11B - Infantry)? _____

2. What is your rank (e.g., O-3, E-6)? _____

3. What is your current duty position (e.g., company commander)? _____

4. How long have you been in your current duty position? _____ years _____ months

5. Please circle the type of **BRIGADE** that you currently serve in:
   a. Brigade Combat Team (BCT)
   b. Functional Brigade
   c. Multifunctional Brigade

6. Please circle the type of **BATTALION** that you currently serve in:
   a. Infantry   d. Field Artillery   g. Recon   j. Other:
   b. Armor   e. BEB   h. Engineer   _____
   c. Stryker   f. BSB   i. Medical

7. Please circle the statement that best describes your **CURRENT** situation.
   a. Just returned (within 3 months) from deployment
   b. Preparing for a deployment within the next 6 months
   c. In - between deployments

8. Think back to **YESTERDAY**, how long did you work (including PT and evenings)?
   _____ hours _____ mins

9. Think back over the **LAST MONTH**, how many hours **PER WEEK** did you usually work (including PT and evenings)? _____ hours

10. Think back over the **LAST MONTH**, during a **TYPICAL WEEK**,
    a. ...how many hours did you personally spend in and preparing for **NON-MISSION ESSENTIAL** meetings?
       BN level meetings: _____ hours
       CO level meetings: _____ hours

Please circle your level of agreement or disagreement with the following statement:

11. The amount of time your job takes up makes it difficult to fulfill non-work responsibilities [home, family, social].   Strongly disagree   Disagree   Agree   Strongly agree

↳ If you answered agree or strongly agree, how many **FEWER** hours **PER WEEK** working would you want to achieve better work-life balance? _____ hours

12. What outlets do you commonly read for Army-related information? (e.g., RallyPoint, Duffle Blog, Company Command Forum): _____
    _____

STOP FOR DISCUSSION

SECTION B: Job Tasks in Garrison

We are interested in YOUR time, not your unit's time

General Job Tasks and Examples	During a TYPICAL QUARTER, estimate how much time (in percentages) you spend on each task category.
■ **Higher Command**	*It's OK if the percentages do not total 100 exactly!*
1 -**Taskings**	
-Distinguished visitors	
-Inspections (DAIG, CSA / SA directed and others)	
-OPFOR / External evaluation support to include CTCs	_____%
-Operational testing support / NET / DTT / NIE / AWA	
-"Umbrella Weeks" (e.g., call)	
-Red cycles taskings	
2 -**Meetings**	_____%
- Command and Staff / Cyclic Training Briefs /Battalion training meetings	
3 ■ **AR 350-1 (Mandatory Army-Wide Training)** Self and Other	
- HQDA Mandatory Training *(OPSEC, substance abuse, equal opportunity, antiterrorism, SHARP, composite risk management, information security training, suicide prevention, values, disease prevention training, law of war/ detainee ops, human trafficking, personnel recovery, TARP)*	_____%
4 ■ **Unit-Specific Training**	
-Company training meetings	_____%
-Unit-collective training / Joint and Army exercises / Assigned force missions / Regionally aligned force alignment tasks	
-Supporting individual training	
-8 step training model / recovery	
-EIB / EFMB / EIA / Warrior Task & Battle Drills	
5 ■ **AR 600-20 (Army Command Policy)**	_____%
-UCMJ enforcement / dealing with high-risk Soldiers	
-Health, welfare, and morale, etc. (daily PT & APFT admin.)	
-Family Readiness	
-Unit functions / changes of command / award ceremonies	
-Administration of individual leave / pass / compensatory time	
-Organizational Inspection Program	
-Pay Day activities / performance counseling	
6 ■ **Tracking Readiness (Personnel and Training)**	_____%
-IDES / MEDPROS / Resiliency / PAI / SRP/ DTMS	
7 ■ **Self-Development**	_____%
-Professional Military Education / Functional Training (Schools)/ Civilian Education	
-Foreign Language Proficiency Testing	
-Leader development programs	
8 ■ **Equipment Maintenance and Accountability**	
-Inventories (cyclic / sensitive item)	_____%
-Command maintenance / services (supervising maintenance, submitting and reviewing parts requests)	
9 ■ **Installation Support**	
-Borrowed Military Manpower	
-Funerals / retirement ceremonies/ gate guards / crossing guards / range support	_____%
-Cleaning post	
-Community outreach	
■ **Other – Describe briefly.**	_____%

STOP FOR DISCUSSION

SECTION C: Job Resources

Job Resources	How IMPORTANT is each resource to helping you perform your current tasks?				What is the current AVAILABILITY of each resource?		
	Not at all important [1]	Slightly important [2]	Moderately Important [3]	Very important [4]	Too little [1]	About right [2]	Too much [3]
SUPPORT							
■ **Informal Mentorship** You have access to individuals who ARE NOT in your current chain of command who provide helpful guidance that contributes to your work performance and/or general well-being	1	2	3	4	1	2	3
■ **Command Support** Your commanders provide helpful guidance that contributes to your work performance and/or general well-being	1	2	3	4	1	2	3
■ **Peer Support** There are individuals in similar job positions as you who contribute to your work performance and/or general well-being	1	2	3	4	1	2	3
■ **Delegation** Your Soldiers can effectively meet your intent in completing taskings	1	2	3	4	1	2	3
■ **Family Support** Your family (e.g., significant other, children, parents, siblings) are understanding of your work obligations	1	2	3	4	1	2	3
ENABLERS							
■ **Technology Tools** You have access to and understanding of Information Technology (IT) tools that contribute to your work performance	1	2	3	4	1	2	3
■ **Formal Training** You have received the appropriate formal training to perform your job tasks	1	2	3	4	1	2	3
■ **Role Clarity** You know the expectations and standards of your position	1	2	3	4	1	2	3
■ **Autonomy** As long as the commander's intent is met, you can determine:							
(a) which tasks are performed	1	2	3	4	1	2	3
(b) how tasks are accomplished	1	2	3	4	1	2	3
REINFORCEMENT							
■ **Recognition** You are recognized for your contributions, either through formal or informal means (e.g., awards or compliments)	1	2	3	4	1	2	3
■ **Performance Feedback** You receive regular & constructive feedback on your performance from your leadership and/or the job itself	1	2	3	4	1	2	3
■ **Other**							

STOP FOR DISCUSSION

NOTES: AWA = Army Warfighting Assessment; BEB = brigade engineer battalion; BSB = brigade support battalion; CSA = Chief of Staff of the Army; DAIG = Department of Army Inspector General; DTMS = Digital Training Management System; DTT = Doctrine Training Team; EFMB = Expert Field Medical Badge; EIA = Environmental Impact Analysis; EIB = Experty Infantryman Badge; IDES = Integrated Disability Evaluation System; MEDPROS = Medical Protection System; MOS = Military Occupational Specialty; NET = new equipment training; NIE = Network Integration Evaluation; OPSEC = Operations Security; PAI = Personnel Asset Inventory; SA = Secretary of the Army; SRP = Sustainable Range Program; UCMJ = Uniform Code of Military Justice.

Bibliography

Abernathy, Donna J., "A Get-Real Guide to Time Management," *Training and Development*, June 1999, pp. 22–26.

Abramis, David J., "Work Role Ambiguity, Job Satisfaction, and Job Performance: Meta-Analyses and Review," *Psychological Reports*, Vol. 75, No. 3_suppl, 1994, pp. 1411–1433. As of July 15, 2019: https://doi.org/10.2466/pr0.1994.75.3f.1411

Abrams, Robert B., Commanding General, Headquarters, U.S. Army Forces Command, Department of the Army, "FORSCOM Command Training Guidance (CTG)—Fiscal Year 2018," memorandum to commanders, major subordinate commands/units reporting directly to FOSRCOM; Army National Guard (ARNG) Bureau; Office of the Chief, Army Reserve; and Army Service Component Commands (ASCC), Fort Bragg, N.C., March 24, 2017.

Abu Elanain, Hossam M., "Job Characteristics, Work Attitudes and Behaviors in a Non-Western Context: Distributive Justice as a Mediator," *Journal of Management Development*, Vol. 28, No. 5, 2009, pp. 457–477.

Adams, Gary A., and Steve M. Jex, "Relationships Between Time Management, Control, Work-Family Conflict, and Strain," *Journal of Occupational Health Psychology*, Vol. 4, No. 1, 1999, pp. 72–77.

Adler, Rachel F., and Raquel Benbunan-Fich, "Juggling on a High Wire: Multitasking Effects on Performance," *International Journal of Human-Computer Studies*, Vol. 70, No. 2, February 2012, pp. 156–168.

ADP—*See* Army Doctrine Publication.

Akiva, Thomas, Junlei Li, Kelly M. Martin, Christy Galletta Horner, and Anne R. McNamara, "Simple Interactions: Piloting a Strengths-Based and Interaction-Based Professional Development Intervention for Out-of-School Time Programs," *Child & Youth Care Forum*, Vol. 46, No. 3, June 2017, pp. 285–305.

Alarcon, Gene M., "A Meta-Analysis of Burnout with Job Demands, Resources, and Attitudes," *Journal of Vocational Behavior*, Vol. 79, No. 2, October 2011, pp. 549–562.

Albritton, Rob, "Four Steps the Department of Defense Can Take to Fix Its Broken Personnel System," *War on the Rocks*, December 21, 2015. As of February 5, 2018:
https://warontherocks.com/2015/12/four-steps-the-department-of-defense-can-take-to-fix-its-broken-personnel-system/

Allen, Natalie J., and John P. Meyer, "The Measurement and Antecedents of Affective, Continuance and Normative Commitment to the Organization," *Journal of Occupational Psychology*, Vol. 63, No. 1, March 1990, pp. 1–18.

Alwine, Rebecca, "Spouses Balance Work, Family, Army," *ARMY Magazine*, June 2016, pp. 56–57.

Amberg, John W., II, "Set 'Em Up for Success," *Field Artillery*, Vol. 3, May–June 1999, pp. 38–39.

Ancona, Deborah G., Paul S. Goodman, Barbara S. Lawrence, and Michael L. Tushman, "Time: A New Research Lens," *Academy of Management Review*, Vol. 26, No. 4, October 2001, pp. 645–663.

Anderson, Gina, "Carving Out Time and Space in the Managerial University," *Journal of Organizational Change Management*, Vol. 19, No. 5, 2006, pp. 578–592.

"Are Customs and Courtesies Important in Today's Army?" *ARMY Magazine*, Vol. 61, No. 12, December 2011, pp. 65–69.

Ariely, Daniel, and Klaus Wertenbroch, "Procrastination, Deadlines, and Performance: Self-Control by Precommitment," *Psychological Science*, Vol. 13, No. 3, May 2002, pp. 219–224. As of July 15, 2019:
https://doi.org/10.1111/1467-9280.00441

Army Directive 2016-05, *Building Training Readiness*, Washington, D.C.: Secretary of the Army, February 11, 2016.

Army Directive 2018-07-8, *Prioritizing Efforts—Readiness and Lethality (Update 8)*, Washington, D.C.: Secretary of the Army, June 4, 2018.

Army Doctrine Publication No. 6-0, *Mission Command*, Washington, D.C.: Headquarters, Department of the Army, May 2012.

Army Doctrine Publication No. 7-0, *Training Units and Developing Leaders*, Washington, D.C.: Headquarters, Department of the Army, August 23, 2016.

Army Doctrine Publication No. 7-0, *Training*, Washington, D.C.: Headquarters, Department of the Army, August 29, 2018. As of July 17, 2019:
https://armypubs.army.mil/epubs/DR_pubs/DR_a/pdf/web/ARN12051_ADP%207-0%20FINAL%20WEB.pdf

Army Regulation 350-1, *Army Training and Leader Development*, Washington, D.C.: Headquarters, Department of the Army, December 10, 2017.

Army Regulation 385-10, *The Army's Safety Program*, Washington, D.C.: Headquarters, Department of the Army, February 24, 2017.

Army Regulation 525-28, *Personnel Recovery*, Washington, D.C.: Headquarters, Department of the Army, March 5, 2010.

Army Regulation 570-4, *Manpower Management*, Washington, D.C.: Headquarters, Department of the Army, February 8, 2006.

Army Regulation 600-20, *Army Command Policy*, Washington, D.C.: Headquarters, Department of the Army, November 6, 2014.

Army Regulation 600-38, *The Meal Card Management System*, Washington, D.C.: Headquarters, Department of the Army, August 17, 2016.

Army Regulation 600-55, *The Army Driver and Operator Standardization Program (Selection, Training, Testing and Licensing)*, Washington, D.C.: Headquarters, Department of the Army, May 1, 2017.

Army Regulation 600-100, *Army Profession and Leadership Policy*, Washington, D.C.: Headquarters, Department of the Army, April 5, 2017.

Army Regulation 710-2, *Supply Policy Below the National Level*, Washington, D.C.: Headquarters, Department of the Army, March 28, 2008.

Arnold, Charles L., "The Need for Cross-Training at the Company Level," *Army Logistician*, Vol. 40, No. 1, January–February 2008, p. 17.

Babbage, Charles, *On the Economy of Machinery and Manufacturers*, London, U.K.: Knight, 1835.

Bakker, Arnold B., "A Job Demands-Resources Approach to Public Service Motivation," *Public Administration Review*, Vol. 75, No. 5, September–October 2015, pp. 723–732.

Bakker, Arnold B., and Evangelia Demerouti, "The Job Demands-Resources Model: State of the Art," *Journal of Managerial Psychology*, Vol. 22, No. 3, April 2007, pp. 309–328.

———, "Job Demands-Resources Theory," in Peter Y. Chen and Cary L. Cooper, eds., *Work and Wellbeing*, Vol. III: *Wellbeing: A Complete Reference Guide*, Hoboken, N.J.: Wiley, 2014.

Bakker, Arnold B., Evangelia Demerouti, and Martin C. Euwema, "Job Resources Buffer the Impact of Job Demands on Burnout," *Journal of Occupational Health Psychology*, Vol. 10, No. 2, April 2005, pp. 170–180.

Bakker, Arnold B., Evangelia Demerouti, and Ana Isabel Sanz-Vergel, "Burnout and Work Engagement: The JD-R Approach," *Annual Review of Organizational Behavior*, Vol. 1, March 2014, pp. 389–411.

Bakker, Arnold B., and Ana Isabel Sanz-Vergel, "Weekly Work Engagement and Flourishing: The Role of Hindrance and Challenge Job Demands," *Journal of Vocational Behavior*, Vol. 83, No. 3, December 2013, pp. 397–409.

Barela, Timothy P., "Attention to Details," *Airman*, Vol. 42, No. 8, August 1998, pp. 40–43.

Barno, David, and Nora Bensahel, "Six Ways to Fix the Army's Culture," *War on the Rocks*, September 6, 2016. As of February 5, 2018: https://warontherocks.com/2016/09/six-ways-to-fix-the-armys-culture/

———, "Three Things the Army Chief of Staff Wants You to Know," *War on the Rocks*, May 23, 2017. As of February 5, 2018: https://warontherocks.com/2017/05/three-things-the-army-chief-of-staff-wants -you-to-know/

Baxter, Timothy S., "Paperwork Is Choking the Reserves," *Proceedings Magazine*, Vol. 66, August 1997.

Beineke, Paul R., *Balancing Time Demands . . . A Vital Strategic Asset*, Carlisle Barracks, Pa.: U.S. Army War College, 2010.

Beirne, Charles J., "Transition to a Total Army Training Plan," *Small Wars Journal*, August 29, 2015.

"The Best Advice I've Ever Received," *ARMY Magazine*, March 2014, pp. 57–61.

"Best Tips, Techniques and Advice on 'Time Management?'" *RallyPoint.com*, January 18, 2014. As of February 5, 2018: https://www.rallypoint.com/answers/best-tips-techniques-advice-on-time -management

Birkinshaw, Julian, and Jordan Cohen, "Make Time for the Work that Matters," *Harvard Business Review*, September 2013, pp.115–118.

Blondesoverbaghdad, "Hardest Working Soldier in Battalion Wins 'More Work' Award," *Duffel Blog*, June 23, 2016. As of July 15, 2019: http://www.duffelblog.com/2016/06/hardest-working-man-battalion-wins -work-award/

Blu, Addison, "Battalion to Hold Sleep Deprivation Awareness Brief at 0430," *Duffel Blog*, June 2016. As of February 5, 2018: http://www.duffelblog.com/2016/06/battalion-sleep-deprivation-awareness-brief/

Bond, Frank W., Paul E. Flaxman, and David Bunce, "The Influence of Psychological Flexibility on Work Redesign: Mediated Moderation of a Work Reorganization Intervention," *Journal of Applied Psychology*, Vol. 93, No. 3, May 2008, pp. 645–654.

Bond, M., and N. Feather, "Some Correlates of Structure and Purpose In the Use of Time," *Journal of Personality and Social Psychology*, Vol. 55, No. 2, August 1988, pp. 321–329.

Boniwell, Ilona, Evgey Osin, and Anna Sircova, "Introducing Time Perspective Coaching: A New Approach to Improve Time Management and Enhance Well-Being," *International Journal of Evidence Based Coaching and Mentoring*, Vol. 12, No. 2, August 2014, pp. 24–40.

Boon, Corine, Frank D. Belschak, Deanne N. Den Hartog, and Mark Pjnenburg, "Perceived Human Resource Management Practices: Their Effect on Employee Absenteeism and Time Allocation at Work," *Journal of Personnel Psychology*, Vol. 13, No. 1, 2014, pp. 21–33.

Borst, Jelmer P., Miels A. Taatgen, and Hedderik van Rijn, "The Problem State: A Cognitive Bottleneck in Multitasking," *Journal of Experimental Psychology: Learning, Memory, and Cognition*, Vol. 36, No. 2, March 2010, pp. 363–382.

Bouchard, Thomas J., Jr., David T. Lykken, Matthew McGue, Nancy L. Segal, and Auke Tellegen, "Sources of Human Psychological Differences: The Minnesota Study of Twins Reared Apart," *Science*, Vol. 250, No. 4978, October 1990, pp. 223–228.

Bount, Sally, and Gregory A. Janicik, "When Plans Change: Examining How People Evaluate Timing Changes in Work," *Academy of Management Review*, Vol. 26, No. 4, October 2001, pp. 566–585.

Branch, Shelley, "So Much Work, So Little Time," *Fortune*, Vol. 135, No. 2, February 3, 1997, pp. 115–117.

Bray, Robert M., Carol S. Camlin, John A. Fairbank, George H. Dunteman, and Sara C. Wheeless, "The Effects of Stress on Job Functioning of Military Men and Women," *Armed Forces and Society*, Vol. 27, No. 3, June 2010, pp. 397–417.

Britt, Thomas W., and Craig R. Dawson, "Predicting Work-Family Conflict from Workload, Job Attitudes, Group Attributes, and Health: A Longitudinal Study," *Military Psychology*, Vol. 17, No. 3, 2005, pp. 203–227.

Britton, Bruce K., and Abraham Tesser, "Effects of Time-Management Practices on College Grades," *Journal of Educational Psychology*, Vol. 83, No. 3, 1991, pp. 405–410.

Brogan, Chris, "The New Attention Deficit," *Entrepreneur*, December 2010, p. 70.

Brown, Ed, "Stephen Covey's New One-Day Seminar," *Fortune*, Vol. 139, No. 2, February 1, 1999, pp. 138–139.

Bruch, Heike, and Sumantra Ghoshal, "Beware the Busy Manager," *Harvard Business Review*, Vol. 80, No. 2, February 2002.

Buchanan, Leigh, "The Psychology of Productivity: Burned Out? Not Enough Hours in the Day? The Problem May Be in Your Head," *Inc.*, March 2015, pp. 50–57.

"Building Combat Ready Teams: The Crush of Requirements from Higher Headquarters," *ARMY Magazine*, Vol. 62, No. 8, August 2012, pp. 53–57.

Burke, Crispin J., "No Time, Literally, for All Requirements," *ARMY Magazine*, April 2016, pp. 16–17.

————, "Computer Driving You Crazy? Six Ways to Prevent Junior Leaders from Drowning in Data," *Association of the United States Army*, May 15, 2017. As of February 5, 2018:
https://www.ausa.org/articles/prevent-junior-leaders-drowning-data

Burke, Crispin, James King, and Niel Smith, "Abort, Retry, Fail? Fixing Army Software," *Small Wars Journal*, 2013.

Burlingham, Donald M., "Resource Allocation: A Practical Example," *Marine Corps Gazette*, Vol. 85, No. 1, January 2001, pp. 60–64.

Burnett, Alexander, "New Spin on Old Training Gives SHARP an Edge," *Federal News Service*, May 16, 2014.

Burr, Renu, and John L. Cordery, "Self-Management Efficacy As A Mediator of the Relation Between Job Design and Employee Motivation," *Human Performance*, Vol. 14, No. 1, 2001, pp. 27–44.

Burroughs, Mikel, "Do You Use Time Management Practices to Be Become More Productive Leaders?" *RallyPoint.com*, July 15, 2015. As of February 5, 2018:
https://www.rallypoint.com/answers/do-you-use-time-management-practices-to
-be-become-more-productive-leaders?loc=similar_mainandpos=1andtype=qrc

————, "What Training Creates Great Leaders?" *RallyPoint.com*, May 23, 2016. As of February 5, 2018:
https://www.rallypoint.com/answers/what-training-creates-great-leaders

Burt, Christopher D.B., Alexandra Westrate, Caroline Brown, and Felicity Champion, "Development of the Time Management Environment (TiME) Scale," *Journal of Managerial Psychology*, Vol. 25, No. 6, September 2010, pp. 649–668.

Calonius, Erik, "How Top Managers Manage Their Time," *Fortune*, June 4, 1990.

Cammann, Cortlandt, Mark Fichman, G. Douglas Jenkins, and John Klesh, "Michigan Organizational Assessment Questionnaire," in Stanley E. Seashore, Edward E. Lawler, Philip H. Mirvis, and Cortlandt Cammann, eds., *Assessing Organizational Change: A Guide To Methods, Measures, and Practices*, New York: Wiley-Interscience, 1983, pp. 71–138.

Campbell, Donald W., "The Privatization of Military Training Would Benefit U.S.," *National Defense*, Vol. 87, No. 588, November 2002, pp. 70–71.

Campion, Michael A., "Interdisciplinary Approaches to Job Design: A Constructive Replication with Extensions," *Journal of Applied Psychology*, Vol. 73, No. 3, August 1988, pp. 467–481.

Campion, Michael A., and Paul W. Thayer, "Development and Field Evaluation of an Interdisciplinary Measure of Job Design," *Journal of Applied Psychology*, Vol. 70, No. 1, 1985, pp. 29–43.

Cappelli, Peter, and J. R. Keller, "Classifying Work in the New Economy," *Academy of Management Review*, Vol. 38, No. 4, October 2013, pp. 575–596.

Caraccilo, Dominic J., "Micromanagement Can Cripple a Command," *ARMY Magazine*, Vol. 65, No. 12, December 2015, pp. 25–26.

Carafano, James Jay, "Military Needs Should Drive Personnel Reforms," *ARMY Magazine*, Vol. 66, No. 9, September 2016, pp. 8–9.

Carbonara, Peter, "Sleep Is for Wusses," *Inc.*, Vol. 20, No. 4, 1998, p. 29.

Carey, John N., "So You Want to Be a Company Commander?" *Engineer*, April–June 2008, pp. 49–53.

Carise, Deni, Meghan Love, Julia Zur, A. Thomas McLellan, and Jack Kemp, "Results of a State-Wide Evaluation of 'Paperwork Burden' in Addiction Treatment," *Journal of Substance Abuse Treatment*, Vol. 37, No. 1, July 2009, pp. 101–109.

Carlson, Jessica H., and Steven Mellor, "Gender-Related Effects in the Job-Design–Job-Satisfaction Relationship: An Interactional Approach," *Sex Roles*, Vol. 51, No. 3–4, pp. 237–247.

Carver, Charles S., and Michael F. Scheier, "Control Theory: A Useful Conceptual Framework for Personality-Social, Clinical, and Health Psychology," *Psychological Bulletin*, Vol. 92, No. 1, August 1982, pp. 111–135.

Cat Astronaut, "Major Pokes Head out of Meeting, Predicts 6 More Hours of Useless Slides," *Duffel Blog*, February 2017. As of February 5, 2018: http://www.duffelblog.com/2017/02/groundhog-day-pentagon/

Cavallaro, Gina, "Constructive Criticism," *Army Times*, May 4, 2009.

Cavanaugh, Marcie A., Wendy R. Boswell, Mark V. Roehling, and John W. Boudreau, "An Empirical Examination of Self-Reported Work Stress Among U.S. Managers," *Journal of Applied Psychology*, Vol. 85, No. 1, 2000, pp. 65–74.

Chaney, Edward, "Managing a Micromanager," *Inc.*, Vol. 27, No. 4, April 2005, p. 50.

Chen, C., and S. Chiu, "The Mediating Role of Job Involvement in the Relationship Between Job Characteristics and Organizational Citizenship Behavior," *Journal of Social Psychology*, Vol. 149, 2009, pp. 474–494.

Chen, Jiaqiong, and Ronald G. Askin, "Project Selection, Scheduling and Resource Allocation with Time Dependent Returns," *European Journal of Operation Research*, Vol. 193, 2009, pp. 23–34.

Cherns, A., "The Principles of Sociotechnical Design," *Human Relations*, Vol. 29, 1978, pp. 783–792.

Cho, Kit W., Jeanette Altarriba, and Maximilian Popiel, "Mental Juggling: When Does Multitasking Impair Reading Comprehension?" *Journal of General Psychology*, Vol. 142, No. 2, 2015, pp. 90–105.

Claessens, Brigitte J.C., Wendelien van Eerde, Christel G. Rutte, and Robert A. Roe, "Planning Behavior and Perceived Control of Time at Work," *Journal of Organizational Behavior*, Vol. 25, No. 8, 2004, pp. 937–950.

———, "A Review of the Time Management Literature," *Personnel Review*, Vol. 36, No. 2, 2007, pp. 256–276.

———, "Things to Do Today. . . . A Daily Diary Study on Task Completion at Work," *Applied Psychology: An International Review*, Vol. 59, No. 2, 2010, pp. 273–295.

Clarity, Tom, "Hardware, Not Humans: The U.S. Navy's History of Technology and Micro-Management," *Small Wars Journal*, 2015.

Clifton, Donald O., and James K. Harter, "Investing in Strengths," in Kim S. Cameron, James E. Dutton, and Robert E. Quinn, eds., *Positive Organizational Scholarship: Foundations of a New Discipline*, San Francisco, Calif.: Berrett-Koehler, 2003, pp. 111–121.

Conger, Jay A., and Rabindra N. Kanungo, "The Empowerment Process: Integrating Theory and Practice," *Academy of Management Review*, Vol. 13, No. 3, 1988, pp. 471–482.

Connelly, Julie, "All Together Now," *Gallup Management Journal*, Vol. 2, 2002, pp. 12–18.

Costello, R., and S. A. Welch, "A Qualitative Analysis of Faculty and Student Perceptions of Effective Online Class Communities Using Herzberg's Motivator-Hygiene Factors," *Quarterly Review of Distance Education*, Vol. 15, 2014, pp. 15–23.

Coviello, Decio, Andrea Ichina, and Nicola Persico, "Time Allocation and Task Juggling," *American Economic Review*, Vol. 104, No. 2, 2014, pp. 609–623.

Crawford, Eean R., Jeffery A. LePine, and Bruce Louis Rich, "Linking Job Demands and Resources to Employee Engagement and Burnout: A Theoretical Extension and Meta-Analytic Test," *Journal of Applied Psychology*, Vol. 95, No. 5, 2010, pp. 834–848.

Crintea, Emil, "Time Management—Ideas to Improve Time Usage in a Military Unit," *Defense Resources Management in the 21st Century: The 7th Scientific Conference with International Attendance*, Brasov, Romania: National Defense University "Carol I" Publishing, November 2012.

Croce, Pat, "Mission: Accomplishment," *Fortune Small Business*, Vol. 15, No. 2, March 2005, pp. 32–33.

Crosby, Cassandra, and Anthony Marston, "Winning in a Complex World Starts with Thinking," *Small Wars Journal*, 2015.

Crossan, Mary, Miguel Pina E. Cunha, Dusya Vera, and João Cunha, "Time and Organizational Improvisation," *Academy of Management Review*, Vol. 30, No. 1, 2005, pp. 129–145.

Cutler, Gale, "Craig Takes Crash Course in Time Management," *Research-Technology Management*, Vol. 48, No. 6, 2005, pp. 57–60.

Davis, L. E., and J. C. Taylor, "Overview," in L. E. Davis and J. C. Taylor, eds., *Design of Jobs*, 2nd ed., Santa Monica, Calif.: Goodyear, 1979, pp. x–xxi.

Degen, E. J., and John W. Spencer, "Challenging Army Force Design," *Small Wars Journal*, 2014.

"Delegate, Delegate, Delegate," *Inc.*, Vol. 31, No. 7, September 2009, p. 132.

Demerouti, Evangelia, Arnold B. Bakker, and Jonathan R. B. Halbesleben, "Productive and Counterproductive Job Crafting: A Daily Diary Study," *Journal of Occupational Health Psychology*, Vol. 20, 2015, pp. 457–469.

Demerouti, Evangelia, Arnold B. Bakker, F. Nachreiner, and W. B. Schaufeli, "The Job Demands-Resources Model of Burnout," *Journal of Applied Psychology*, Vol. 86, 2001, pp. 499–512.

Demos, Telis, "Stelios Haji-Iaonnou," *Fortune International (Europe)*, Vol. 153, No. 5, March 20, 2006, p. 48.

Department of Defense Instruction 1332.45, *Retention Determinations for Non-Deployable Service Members*, Washington, D.C.: U.S. Office of the Under Secretary of Defense for Personnel and Readiness, July 30, 2018. As of July 17, 2019: http://www.esd.whs.mil/Portals/54/Documents/DD/issuances/dodi/133245p.pdf?ver=2018-08-01-080044-667

Deutschman, Alan, "The CEO's Secret of Managing Time," *Fortune*, Vol. 125, No. 11, June 1, 1992, p. 135.

Devenny, Patrick, "All Available Tools: Parallel Governance and Modern Insurgencies," *Small Wars Journal*, 2009.

Dickstein, Corey, "Mattis Targets Mandatory Training in Effort to Become More Lethal," *Stars and Stripes*, July 26, 2017. As of February 5, 2018: https://www.stripes.com/news/mattis-targets-mandatory-training-in-effort-to-become-more-lethal-1.479980

Dilanian, Arpi, and Matthew Howard, "Back to the Fundamentals: An Interview with Lt. Gen. Joseph Anderson," *Army Sustainment*, March–April 2017.

Dirty, "Fort Bragg Cancels July 4th Passes, Implements Mandatory 'Self-Awareness' Training," *Duffel Blog*, July 2015. As of February 5, 2018: http://www.duffelblog.com/2015/07/fort-bragg-cancels-july-4th/

"Do You Follow a Stupid Order?" *ARMY Magazine*, Vol. 60, No. 93, March 2010, pp. 106–113.

DoD Instruction—*See* Department of Defense Instruction.

Doef, M., and D. Maes, "The Leiden Quality of Work Questionnaire: Its Construction, Factor Structure, and Psychometric Qualities," *Psychological Reports*, Vol. 85, 1999, pp. 954–962.

Donlon, Brian, "Where's the Special Trust and Confidence?" *Proceedings Magazine*, Vol. 135, No. 11, November 2009, pp. 34–38.

Donovan, J. J., and D. J. Radosevich, "A Meta-Analytic Review of the Distribution of Practice Effect: Now You See It, Now You Don't," *Journal of Applied Psychology*, Vol. 84, No. 5, October 1999, pp. 795–805.

Dorr, Robert F., "Time to Review 'Mandatory Fun,'" *Air Force Times*, November 14, 2011, p. 4.

Doty, Joe, and Jeff Fenlason, "Narcissism and Toxic Leaders," *Military Review*, January–February 2013, pp. 55–60.

Doty, Joe, and Pete Hoffman, "Admit It—Lying Is a Problem in the Military," *ARMY Magazine*, July 2014, pp. 19–21.

Dubik, James M., "On Becoming a Strategic Leader," *ARMY Magazine*, Vol. 63, No. 1, January 2013, pp. 16–18.

Duffy, Ryan D., Carrie L. Torrey, Elizabeth M. Bott, Blake A. Allan, and Lewis Z. Schlosser, "Time Management, Passion, and Collaboration: A Qualitative Study of Highly Research Productive Counseling Psychologists," *The Counseling Psychologist*, Vol. 41, No. 6, 2013, pp. 881–917.

Dunham, R. B., "Relationships of Perceived Job Design Characteristics to Job Ability Requirements and Job Value," *Journal of Applied Psychology*, Vol. 62, 1977, pp. 760–763.

Eagleman, David M., "Using Time Perception to Measure Fitness for Duty," *Military Psychology*, Vol. 21, Suppl. 1, 2009, pp. S123–S129.

Editorial Board, "The Navy's McCain Moment: Are U.S. Sailors Being Pushed into Missions Without Enough Training?" *Wall Street Journal*, August 21, 2017. As of February 5, 2018:
https://www.wsj.com/articles/the-navys-mccain-moment-1503354892

Elsbach, K. D., and A. B. Hargadon, "Enhancing Creativity Through 'Mindless' Work: A Framework of Workday Design," *Organization Science*, Vol. 17, 2006, pp. 470–483.

English, Gary, "Beating the Clock: Time to Review Time-Management Training," *Training and Development Journal*, January 1989, pp. 77–79.

Erdoes, Mary Callahan, "5 Tips for Getting It All Done," *ForbesLife*, Vol. 180, October 8, 2007, p. 109.

Eriksson-Zetterquist, Ulla, Tomas Müllern, and Alexander Styhre, *Organization Theory: A Practice Based Approach*, Oxford, U.K.: Oxford University Press, 2011.

Feather, N. T., and K. A. Rauter, "Organizational Citizenship Behaviors in Relation to Job Status, Job Insecurity, Organizational Commitment and Identification, Job Satisfaction and Work Values," *Journal of Occupational and Organizational Psychology*, Vol. 77, 2004, pp. 81–94.

Ferris, Timothy, "The 4-Hour Workweek," *Fortune Small Business*, Vol. 17, No. 4, May 2006, pp. 47–48.

Fisher, Anne, "How to Manage as a First-Time Boss," *Fortune*, Vol. 150, No. 7, October 4, 2004, p. 58.

Fisher, C. D., and R. Gitelson, "A Meta-Analysis of the Correlates of Role Conflict and Ambiguity," *Journal of Applied Psychology*, Vol. 68, No. 2, 1983, pp. 320–333. As of July 15, 2019:
http://dx.doi.org/10.1037/0021-9010.68.2.320

Foltz-Gray, Dorothy, "Mind/Balance Makeover," *Health*, Vol. 18, No. 9, November 2004, pp. 102–106. As of July 15, 2019:
http://www.exitstageright.com/news/2004-health.htm

Ford, R. N., *Motivation Through the Work Itself*, New York: American Management Association, 1969.

FORSCOM—*See* U.S. Army Forces Command.

Forsyth, Darryl K., and Bevan Catley, "Time Management and the Full-Time Sportsperson: Increasing Individual Perceptions of Time Control," *International Journal of Sports Science and Coaching*, Vol. 2, No. 3, 2007, pp. 305–317.

Fortunato, V. J., and E. F. Stone-Romero, "Positive Affectivity as a Moderator of the Objective-Task Characteristics/Perceived-Task Characteristics Relationship," *Journal of Applied Social Psychology*, Vol. 31, 2001, pp. 1248–1278.

French, Brent, and Steven Kauffman, "Decision Framework for Dynamic Manpower Reallocation," *Air Force Journal of Logistics*, Vol. 30/31, No. 4/1, Winter 2006–Spring 2007, pp. 112–115.

Freund, William A., "How Military Intelligence NCOs Develop Training: A Pragmatic Approach," *Military Intelligence Professional Bulletin*, January–March 2017, pp. 21–24.

Fried, Jason, "Letting Go," *Inc.*, Vol. 35, No. 5, June 2013, p. 128.

———, "In Praise of Deadlines," *Inc.*, December–January 2015–2016, p. 128.

Fried, Y., and G. R. Ferris, "The Validity of the Job Characteristics Model: A Review and Meta-Analysis," *Personnel Psychology*, Vol. 40, 1987, pp. 287–322.

Fukuzawa, Mathew, "Processing Leader Development," *Small Wars Journal*, 2016.

Gallagher, Leigh, "How I Managed My Time—the Covey Way," *Fortune*, Vol. 163, No. 4, March 21, 2011, pp. 39–40.

GAO—*See* U.S. Government Accountability Office.

Garaus, Christian, Wolfgang H. Guttel, Stefan Konlechner, Irina Koprax, Hubert Lackner, Karin Link, and Barbara Muller, "Bridging Knowledge in Ambidextrous HRM Systems: Empirical Evidence from Hidden Champion," *International Journal of Human Resource Management*, Vol. 27, No. 3, 2016, pp. 355–381.

Gardner, Heidi K., "Performance Pressure as a Double-Edged Sword: Enhancing Team Motivation but Undermining the Use of Team Knowledge," *Administrative Science Quarterly*, Vol. 57, No. 1, 2012, pp. 1–46.

Gaskin, James E., and Tanner Skousen, "Time-Chunking and Hyper-Refocusing in a Digitally-Enabled Workplace: Six Forms of Knowledge Workers," *Frontiers in Psychology*, Vol. 7, No. 1627, October 2016. As of July 15, 2019: https://pdfs.semanticscholar.org/95d8/d83a897562c446c39817ffdf29351895fe67 .pdf

Gauthier, H. Lucien, III, "Tacit Knowledge and Hybrid Sailors," *U.S. Naval Institute Blog*, December 5, 2010. As of February 5, 2018: https://blog.usni.org/posts/2010/12/05/9310

———, "Guest Post: Viewed From the Deckplates," *U.S. Naval Institute Blog*, June 26, 2011. As of February 5, 2018: https://blog.usni.org/posts/2011/06/26/guest-post-viewed-from-the-deckplates

Gawande, Atul, *The Checklist Manifesto: How to Get Things Right*, New York: Metropolitan Books, 2009.

Gayton, S. Jamie, *The Effect of Knowledge Management Systems on Organizational Performance: Do Soldier and Unit Counterinsurgency Knowledge and Performance Improve Following "Push" or "Adaptive-Push" Training?* dissertation, Pardee RAND Graduate School, Santa Monica, Calif.: RAND Corporation, RGSD-246, 2009. As of July 15, 2019: https://www.rand.org/pubs/rgs_dissertations/RGSD246.html

Gersick, Connie J. G., "Time and Transition in Work Teams: Toward a New Model of Group Development," *Academy of Management Journal*, Vol. 31, No. 1, 1988, pp. 9–41.

Gibson, Cristina B., and Julian Birkinshaw, "The Antecedents, Consequences, and Mediating Role of Organizational Ambidexterity," *Academy of Management Journal*, Vol. 47, No. 2, 2004, pp. 209–226.

Glick, W. H., G. D. Jenkins, and N. Gupta, "Method Versus Substance: How Strong Are Underlying Relationships Between Job Characteristics and Attitudinal Outcomes?" *Academy of Management Journal*, Vol. 29, 1986, pp. 441–464.

Goodman, Michelle, "Bootstrap Your Business," *Entrepreneur*, December 2011, pp. 90–95.

———, "Entrepreneurial Zen," *Entrepreneur*, September 2013, pp. 88–90.

Grant, A. M., "The Significance of Task Significance: Job Performance Effects, Relational Mechanisms, and Boundary Conditions," *Journal of Applied Psychology*, Vol. 93, 2008, pp. 108–124.

Grant, Adam M., and Sharon K. Parker, "Redesigning Work Design Theories: The Rise of Relational and Proactive Perspectives," Academy of Management Annals, Vol. 3, 2009, pp. 317–375.

Gray, Wayne D., Chris R. Sims, Wai-Tat Fu, and Michael J. Schoelles, "The Soft Constraints Hypothesis: A Rational Analysis Approach to Resource Allocation for Interactive Behavior," *Psychological Review*, Vol. 113, No. 3, 2006, pp. 461–482.

Green, Peter, and Denise Skinner, "Does Time Management Training Work? An Evaluation," *International Journal of Training and Development*, Vol. 9, No. 2, 2005, pp. 124–139.

Gresov, C., "Designing Organizations to Innovate and Implement: Using Two Dilemmas to Create a Solution," *Columbia Journal of World Business*, Vol. 19, No. 4, 1984, pp. 63–67.

Hackman, J. R., "Work Design," in J. R. Hackman and J. L. Suttle, eds., *Improving Life at Work: Behavioral Science Approaches to Organizational Change*, Pacific Palisades, Calif.: Goodyear, 1976.

Hackman, J. Richard, and Greg R. Oldham, *The Job Diagnostic Survey: An Instrument For the Diagnosis of Jobs and the Evaluation of Job Redesign Projects*, New Haven, Conn.: Yale University Department of Administrative Sciences, Report No. TR-4, 1974.

———, "Development of the Job Diagnostic Survey," *Journal of Applied Psychology*, Vol. 60, 1975, pp. 159–170.

———, "Motivation Through the Design of Work: Test of a Theory," *Organizational Behavior and Human Performance*, Vol. 16, 1976, pp. 250–279.

———, *Work Redesign*, Reading, Mass.: Addison-Wesley, 1980.

Häfner, Alexander, Armin Stock, Lydia Pinneker, and Sabine Strohle, "Stress Prevention Through a Time Management Training Intervention: An Experimental Study," *Educational Psychology*, Vol. 34, No. 3, 2014, pp. 403–416.

Harnish, Verne, "Five Ways to Get Organized," *Fortune*, Vol. 170, No. 3, September 1, 2014, p. 42.

Hawkins, Caitlin, Richard Bowman, Rick Eden, Kristy Gonzalez Morganti, Patrick Grady, Arthur Lackey, and Matthew W. Lewis, unpublished RAND Corporation research, 2010.

Heard, Wayne, "Battalion Management Taught by One of the Best," *ARMY Magazine*, June 2017, pp. 10–12.

Hensrud, Donald D., "If You're Feeling a Little Pinched . . ." *Fortune*, Vol. 143, No. 7, April 2, 2001, p. 202.

Herzberg, G., B. Mausner, and B. B. Snyderman, *The Motivation to Work*, New York: Wiley, 1959.

Hickey, Amy, "Action Workouts: Doing More with Less," *The Mobility Forum*, Vol. 7, No. 1, January–February 1998, pp. 20–21.

History.com Editors, "Ford's Assembly Line Starts Rolling," *History.com*, November 13, 2009. As of February 5, 2018:
http://www.history.com/this-day-in-history/fords-assembly-line-starts-rolling

Hobfoll, Stevan E., "The Influence of Culture, Community, and the Nested-Self in the Stress Process: Advancing Conservation of Resources Theory," *Applied Psychology*, Vol. 50, No. 3, 2001, pp. 337–421.

Hobfoll, Stevan E., Robert J. Johnson, Nicole Ennis, and Anita P. Jackson, "Resource Loss, Resource Gain, and Emotional Outcomes Among Inner City Women," *Journal of Personality and Social Psychology*, Vol. 84, No. 5, 2005, pp. 632–645.

Hodges, Timothy D., and Donald O. Clifton, "Strengths-Based Development in Practice," in P. Alex Linley and Stephen Joseph, eds., *Positive Psychology in Practice*, Hoboken, N.J.: Wiley, 2004.

Hoge, Sharon King, "My 60-hour Week," *ForbesLife*, Vol. 180, October 8, 2007, pp. 86–93.

Holman, D. J., C. M. Axtell, C. A. Sprigg, P. Totterdell, and T. D. Wall, "The Mediating Role of Job Characteristics in Job Redesign Interventions: A Serendipitous Quasi-Experiment," *Journal of Organizational Behavior*, Vol. 31, 2010, pp. 84–105.

Holman, D., P. Totterdell, C. Axtell, C. Stride, R. Port, R. Svensson, and L. Zibarraas, "Job Design and the Employee Innovation Process: The Mediating Role of Learning Strategies," *Journal of Business and Psychology*, Vol. 27, 2012, pp. 177–191.

"How to Deal With the Work Load as a Full Time Student in the Army Reserve?" *RallyPoint.com*, April 21, 2015. As of February 5, 2018: https://www.rallypoint.com/answers/how-to-deal-with-the-work-load-as-a-full -time-student-in-the-army-reserve

"How Trust Is Earned or Lost," *ARMY Magazine*, January 2014, pp. 57–61.

Humphry, Stephen E., Jennifer D. Nahrgang, and Frederick P. Morgeson, "Integrating Motivational, Social, and Contextual Work Design Features: A Meta-Analytic Summary and Theoretical Extension of the Work Design Literature," *Journal of Applied Psychology*, Vol. 92, No. 5, 2007, pp. 1332–1356.

Ioannou, Lori, "Stephen Covey on Time Management," *Fortune Small Business*, Vol. 12, No. 5–6, June 2002, p. 73.

Ittleschmerz, M., "A Look Back . . . Discipline in the Navy," *U.S. Naval Institute Blog*, November 4, 2010. As of February 5, 2018: https://blog.usni.org/posts/2010/11/04/a-look-back-discipline-in-the-navy

Jackson, S. E., and R. S. Schuler, "A Meta-Analysis and Conceptual Critique of Research on Role Ambiguity and Role Conflict in Work Settings," *Organizational Behavior and Human Decision Processes*, Vol. 36, No. 1, 1985, pp. 16–78. As of July 15, 2019: http://dx.doi.org/10.1016/0749-5978(85)90020-2

Jaffe, Greg, "Army Worries About 'Toxic' Leaders in Ranks," *Washington Post*, June 25, 2011.

Japenga, Ann, "A Cure for Timesickness," *Health*, Vol. 13, No. 1, January–February 1999, p. 94.

Johnson, Melvin R., II, *Efficacy of SHARP Training in the U.S. Army: A Qualitative Descriptive Single Case Study*, dissertation, University of Phoenix, Phoenix, 2015.

Johnson, Phyllis J., "Development of a Measure of Job Time-Demands," *Psychological Reports*, Vol. 51, 1982, pp. 1087–1094.

Judge, Timothy A., Daniel Heller, and Michael K. Mount, "Five-Factor Model of Personality and Job Satisfaction: A Meta-Analysis," *Journal of Applied Psychology*, Vol. 87, No. 3, pp. 530–541.

"Just Trust," *Inc.*, March 2014, pp. 18–19.

Karasek, R. A., "Job Demands, Job Decision Latitude, and Mental Strain: Implications for Job Redesign," *Administrative Science Quarterly*, Vol. 24, 1979, pp. 285–308.

Karasek, R. A., and T. Theorell, *Healthy Work: Stress, Productivity, and the Reconstruction of Working Life*, New York: Basic Books, 1990.

Karasek, Robert, Chantal Brisson, Norito Kawakami, Irene Houtman, Paulien Bongers, and Benjamin Amick, "The Job Content Questionnaire (JCQ): An Instrument for Internationally Comparative Assessments of Psychosocial Job Characteristics," *Journal of Occupational Health Psychology*, Vol. 3, No. 4, 1998, pp. 322–355.

Kayaalp, Alper, "The Octopus Approach in Time Management: Polychronicity and Creativity," *Military Psychology*, Vol. 24, No. 2, 2014, pp. 67–76.

Kearns, Hugh, and Maria Gardiner, "Is It Time Well Spent? The Relationship Between Time Management Behaviours, Perceived Effectiveness and Work-Related Morale and Distress in a University Context," *Higher Education Research and Development*, Vol. 26, No. 2, 2007, pp. 235–247.

Keegan, Paul, "Get a Life!" *Fortune*, Vol. 158, No. 4, September 1, 2008, pp. 114–120.

Kefalas, Harlan, "Picking Which Ball to Drop," *The Military Leader*, undated. As of February 5, 2018:
http://www.themilitaryleader.com/dropping-the-ball/

———, "Helping Platoon and Company Leaders Juggle," *ARMY Magazine*, June 2017, pp. 8–9.

Kem, Jack, "Focusing on the Critical, Not the Urgent" *Military Intelligence Professional Bulletin*, Vol. 31, No. 3, July–September 2005, pp. 32–35.

Key-Roberts, Melinda, "Strengths-Based Leadership Theory and Development of Subordinate Leaders," *Military Review*, March–April 2014, pp. 4–13.

Kirchberg, Daniela M., Robert A. Roe, and Wendelien van Eerde, "Polychronicity and Multitasking: A Diary Study at Work," *Human Performance*, Vol. 28, 2015, pp. 112–136.

König, C. J., M. Kleinmann, and W. Höhmann, "A Field Test of the Quiet Hour as a Time Management Technique," *Revue Europeenne De Psychologie Appliquee*, Vol. 63, 2013, pp. 137–145.

Kooij, Dorien T. A. M., Marianne van Woerkom, Julia Wilkenloh, Luc Dorenbosch, and Jaap J. A. Denissen, "Job Crafting Towards Strengths and Interests: The Effects of a Job Crafting Intervention on Person-Job Fit and the Role of Age," *Journal of Applied Psychology*, Vol. 102, No. 6, 2017, pp. 971–981.

Kristensen, T. S., H. Hannerz, A. Hogh, and V. Borg, "The Copenhagen Psychosocial Questionnaire—A Tool for the Assessment and Improvement of the Psychosocial Work Environment," *Scandinavian Journal of Work, Environment & Health*, Vol. 31, 2005, pp. 438–449.

Kushner, Kaysi Eastlick, and Margaret J. Harrison, "Employed Mothers: Stress and Balance-Focused Coping," *Canadian Journal of Nursing Research*, Vol. 34, No. 1, 2002, pp. 47–65.

Lammers, Teri, "The Custom-Made Day Planner," *Inc.*, Vol. 14, No. 2, February 1992, p. 61.

Lapowsky, Issie, "Get More Done," *Inc.*, Vol. 35, No. 3, April 2013, pp. 62–70.

Lay, Clarry H., and Henri C. Schouwenburg, "Trait Procrastination, Time Management, and Academic Behavior," *Journal of Social Behavior and Personality*, Vol. 8, No. 4, 1993, pp. 647–662.

Lee, R. L., and B. E. Ashforth, "A Meta-Analytic Examination of the Correlates of the Three Dimensions of Job Burnout," *Journal of Applied Psychology*, Vol. 81, No. 2, 1996, pp. 123–133. As of July 15, 2019: https://doi.org/10.1037//0021-9010.81.2.123

The Leg Ranger, "Breakthrough Military Technology Enables Cutting-Edge Micromanagement," *Duffel Blog*, March 2016. As of February 5, 2018: http://www.duffelblog.com/2016/03/new-technology-cutting-edge -micromanagement/

LePine, Jeffrey A., Nathan P. Podsakoff, and Marcie A. LePine, "A Meta-Analytic Test of the Challenge Stressor-Hindrance Stressor Framework: An Explanation for Inconsistent Relationships Among Stressors and Performance," *Academy of Management Journal*, Vol. 48, No. 5, 2010, pp. 764–775.

Liden, R. C., S. J. Wayne, and R. T. Sparrowe, "An Examination of the Mediating Role of Psychological Empowerment on the Relations Between the Job, Interpersonal Relationships, and Work Outcomes," *Journal of Applied Psychology*, Vol. 85, 2000, pp. 407–416.

Lilley, Kevin, "Report: Officers Are Lying," *Army Times*, March 2, 2015.

Locke, Edwin A., and Gary P. Latham, *A Theory of Goal Setting and Task Performance*, Englewood Cliffs, N.J.: Prentice-Hall, 1990.

Loher, B. T., R. A. Noe, N. L. Moeller, and M. P. Fitzgerald, "A Meta-Analysis of the Relation of Job Characteristics to Job Satisfaction," *Journal of Applied Psychology*, Vol. 70, 1985, pp. 280–289.

Lois, Jennifer, "The Temporal Emotion Work of Motherhood: Homeschoolers' Strategies for Managing Time Shortage," *Gender and Society*, Vol. 24, No. 4, 2010, pp. 421–446.

Lopez, C. Todd, "Milley: Army on Cusp of Profound, Fundamental Change," *Army News Service*, October 6, 2016. As of July 15, 2019: https://www.army.mil/article/176231

———, "Dailey Calls for Recruiting from 'Entire Nation,' Improved Training Opportunities," *Army News Service*, February 17, 2017. As of February 5, 2018: https://www.army.mil/article/182464/dailey_calls_for_recruiting_from_entire _nation_improved_training_opportunities

Lorenz, Stephen R., James A. Hubert, and Keith H. Maxwell, "Linking Resource Allocation to Performance Management and Strategic Planning: An Air Force Challenge," *Aerospace Power Journal*, Vol. 15, No. 4, 2001, pp. 34–45.

Losey, Stephen, "Kelly: Volunteering Won't Help You Get Promoted," *Air Force Times*, July 13, 2015, p. 13.

———, "Air Force Cuts 'Queep' Training Requirements in Half," *Air Force Times*, October 31, 2016. As of February 5, 2018: https://www.airforcetimes.com/news/your-air-force/2016/10/31/air-force-cuts -queep-training-requirements-in-half/

Lytell, Maria C., Susan G. Straus, Chad C. Serena, Geoffrey E. Grimm, James L. Doty III, Jennie W. Wenger, Andrea M. Abler, Andrew M. Naber, Clifford A. Grammich, and Eric S. Fowler, *Assessing Competencies and Proficiency of Army Intelligence Analysts Across the Career Life Cycle*, Santa Monica, Calif.: RAND Corporation, RR-1851-A, 2017. As of July 17, 2019: https://www.rand.org/pubs/research_reports/RR1851.html

Macan, Therese, Janet M. Gibson, and Jennifer Cunningham, "Will You Remember to Read This Article Later When You Have Time? The Relationship Between Prospective Memory and Time Management," *Personality and Individual Differences*, Vol. 48, 2010, pp. 725–730.

Macan, Therese Hoff, "Time Management: Test of a Process Model," *Journal of Applied Psychology*, Vol. 79, No. 3, 1994, pp. 381–391.

———, "Time Management Training: Effects on Time Behaviors, Attitudes, and Job Performance," *The Journal of Psychology*, Vol. 130, No. 3, 1999, pp. 229–236.

Macan, Therese Hoff, Comila Shahani, Robert L. Dipboye, and Amanda Peek Phillips, "College Students' Time Management: Correlations with Academic Performance and Stress," *Journal of Educational Psychology*, Vol. 82, No. 4, 1990, pp. 760–768.

MacDonalds, Jasmine B., Anthony J. Saliba, Gene Hodgins, and Linda A. Ovington, "Burnout in Journalists: A Systematic Literature Review," *Burnout Research*, Vol. 3, 2016, pp. 34–44.

Macquet, Anne-Claire, and Vincent Skalej, "Time Management in Elite Sports: Do Elite Athletes Manage Time Under Fatigue and Stress Conditions?" *Journal of Occupational and Organizational Psychology*, Vol. 88, 2015, pp. 341–363.

Maestas, Nicole, Kathleen J. Mullen, David Powell, Till Von Wachter, and Jeffrey B. Wenger, *Working Conditions in the United States*, Santa Monica, Calif.: RAND Corporation, RR-2014-APSF, 2017. As of February 5, 2018: https://www.rand.org/pubs/research_reports/RR2014.html

Makikangas, Anne, and Ulla Kinnunen, "The Person-Oriented Approach to Burnout: A Systematic Review," *Burnout Research*, Vol. 3, 2016, pp. 11–23.

Mamis, Robert A., "It's Time to Manage Waste," *Inc.*, Vol. 15, No. 1, January 1993, p. 42.

"Mandatory Training," *RallyPoint.com*, November 23, 2013. As of February 5, 2018: https://www.rallypoint.com/answers/mandatory-training

Mankins, Michael, Chris Brahm, and Gregory Caimi, "Your Scarcest Resource," *Harvard Business Review*, May 2014, pp. 74–80.

Marine Corps Order P4790.2C, *MIMMS Field Procedures Manual*, Washington, D.C.: Headquarters, U.S. Marine Corps, 2013.

Maslach, Christina, and Michael P. Leiter, "Early Predictors of Job Burnout and Engagement," *Journal of Applied Psychology*, Vol. 93, No. 3, 2008, pp. 498–512.

Maslach, Christina, Wilmar B. Schaufeli, and Michael P. Leiter, "Job Burnout," *Annual Review of Psychology*, Vol. 52, 2001, pp. 397–422.

Mattis, James N., Secretary of Defense, "Administrative and Personnel Policies to Enhance Readiness and Lethality," memorandum to Secretaries of the Military Departments, Chairman of the Joint Chiefs of Staff, Under Secretaries of Defense, Chiefs of the Military Services, Chief, National Guard Bureau, Commanders of the Combatant Commands, General Counsel of the Department of Defense, Director of Cost Assessment and Program Evaluation, Assistant Secretary of Defense for Legislative Affairs, Washington, D.C., July 21, 2017.

"Maximize Your Day," *Entrepreneur*, July–August 2017, pp. 42–52.

Maylett, Tracy, "6 Ways to Encourage Autonomy with Your Employees," *Entrepreneur*, March 4, 2016. As of July 17, 2019: https://www.entrepreneur.com/article/254030

Mayo, E., *The Human Problems of an Industrial Civilization*, New York: MacMillan, 1933.

———, *The Social Problems of an Industrial Civilization*, Cambridge, MA: Harvard University Press, 1945.

McGirt, Ellen, "Getting out from Under," *Fortune*, Vol. 153, No. 5, March 3, 2006, pp. 88–94.

McGrath, Patrick M., "*Rumsfeld's Rules*: Review," *The Army Lawyer*, February 2014, pp. 29–33.

McIntosh, Robert A., "Ready to Meet Challenges," *The Officer*, Vol. 73, No. 2, February 1997, pp. 54–59.

McNair, Adam, "Overworked," *Air Force Times*, April 20, 2015.

MCO—*See* Marine Corps Order.

Meier, L. L., and P. E. Spector, "Reciprocal Effects of Work Stressors and Counterproductive Work Behavior: A Five-Wave Longitudinal Study," *Journal of Applied Psychology*, Vol. 98, No. 3, 2013, pp. 529–539. As of July 15, 2019: http://dx.doi.org/10.1037/a0031732

Meloy, Guy S., "Training the Trainers—the Arch Carpenter Way," *ARMY Magazine*, May 2008, pp. 55–64.

Meredith, Lisa S., Carra S. Sims, Benjamin Saul Batorsky, Adeyemi Okunogbe, Brittany L. Bannon, and Craig A. Myatt, *Identifying Promising Approaches to U.S. Army Institutional Change*, Santa Monica, Calif.: RAND Corporation, RR-1588-A, 2017. As of July 15, 2019: https://www.rand.org/pubs/research_reports/RR1588.html

Messinger, Leah, "So Time Management Apps Really Make People More Productive?" *The Guardian*, August 18, 2015. As of February 5, 2018: https://www.theguardian.com/business/2015/aug/18/time-management-apps -work-life-balance-productivity

Metz, J. S., "Overtasking and Its Effect on Platoon and Company Tactical Proficienty: An Opposing Forces and Observer/Coach/Trainer Perspective," *Armor: Mounted Maneuver Journal*, Spring 2017. As of February 15, 2018: http://www.benning.army.mil/armor/eARMOR/content/issues/2017/Spring/ 2Metz17.pdf

Meyer, John G., Jr., *Company Command: The Bottom Line*, Washington, D.C.: National Defense University Press, 1990.

Middleton, Melissa, *The Impact of Job Demands and Job Resources on the Burnout and Engagement of Trade Union Representatives*, thesis, Stellenbosch, South Africa: Stellenbosch University, 2017. As of July 15, 2019:
https://scholar.sun.ac.za/handle/10019.1/101215

Minami, Nathan A., *Officer Perceptions of Resource Allocation and Stability in Afghanistan: A Phenomenological Study*, dissertation, Scottsdale, Ariz.: Northcentral University, 2011.

Minkin, Steven, *Air and Space Power Journal*, Vol. 20, No. 4, Winter 2016, pp. 44–51.

Misso, Roger, "Trust, or Trust Not. There Is No 'Verify,'" *U.S. Naval Institute Blog*, December 21, 2015. As of February 5, 2018:
https://blog.usni.org/posts/2015/12/21/trust-or-trust-not-there-is-no-verify

Moeglin, Pierre, and Martine Vidal, "Managing Time, Workload and Costs in Distance Education: Findings from a Literature Review of *Distances Et Mediations Des Savoirs* (formerly *Distances Et Saviors*)," *Distance Education*, Vol. 36, No. 2, 2015, pp. 282–289.

Molinaro, Kristin, "RSLC Cuts Admin Time, Maintains Competitive Edge," *Infantry*, Vol. 98, No. 3, July 2009, p. 46.

Moran, Gwen, "How to Clean up Your Business," *Entrepreneur*, May 2011, pp. 76–78.

Morgenstern, Julie, "Taming the Time Monster," *Fortune Small Business*, Vol. 11, No. 1, 2000, pp. 87–93; originally published in Julie Morgenstern, *Time Management from the Inside Out*, New York: Henry Holt, 2000.

Morgeson, F. P., and M. A. Campion, "Avoiding Tradeoffs When Redesigning Work: Evidence from a Longitudinal Quasi-Experiment," *Personnel Psychology*, Vol. 55, 2002a, pp. 589–612.

———, "Minimizing Tradeoffs When Redesigning Work: Evidence from a Longitudinal Quasi-Experiment," *Personnel Psychology*, Vol. 55, 2002b, pp. 589–612.

———, "Work Design," in W. Borman, R. Klimoski, and D. Ilgen, eds., *Handbook of Psychology*, Vol. 12: *Industrial and Organizational Psychology*, New York: Wiley, 2003, pp. 423–452.

Morgeson, F. P., E. C. Dierdorff, and J. L. Hmurovic, "Work Design in situ: Understanding the Role of Occupational and Organizational Context," *Journal of Organizational Behavior*, Vol. 31, 2010, pp. 351–360.

Morgeson, F. P., A. S. Garza, and M. A. Campion, "Work Design," in Neal W. Schmitt, Scott Highhouse, and Irving B. Weiner, eds., *Handbook of Psychology*, Vol. 12: *Industrial and Organizational Psychology*, 2nd ed., Hoboken, N.J.: Wiley, 2013, pp. 525–559.

Morgeson, F. P., and S. E. Humphrey, "The Work Design Questionnaire (WDQ): Developing and Validating a Comprehensive Measure for Assessing Job Design and the Nature of Work," *Journal of Applied Psychology*, Vol. 91, 2006, pp. 1321–1339.

———, "Job and Team Design: Toward A More Integrative Conceptualization of Work Design," in J. Martocchio, ed., *Research in Personnel and Human Resource Management*, Vol. 27, Bingley, U.K.: Emerald Group Publishing, 2008, pp. 39–91.

Morgeson, F. P., M. D. Johnson, M. A. Campion, G. J. Medsker, and T. V. Mumford, "Understanding Reactions to Job Redesign: A Quasi-Experimental Investigation of the Moderating Effects of Organizational Context on Perceptions of Performance Behavior," *Personnel Psychology*, Vol. 59, 2006, pp. 333–363.

Mudrack, Peter E., "The Structure of Perceptions of Time," *Educational and Psychological Measurement*, Vol. 57, No. 2, 1997, pp. 222–240.

Mullins, Anne Schroeder, "Power Coffee," *ForbesLife*, Vol. 181, Spring 2008, pp. 62–63.

Murphy, Micah, "Addition by Subtraction: Reviewing and Reducing Requirements to Increase Readiness," *Defense360*, December 12, 2016. As of February 5, 2018:
https://defense360.csis.org/reducing-requirements/

Murray, Nicholas, "More Dissent Needed: Critical Thinking and PME," *War on the Rocks*, July 29, 2014. As of February 5, 2018:
https://warontherocks.com/2014/07/more-dissent-needed-critical-thinking-and-pme/

Musso, Michael, "Don't Run in the Pentagon," *Government Executive*, December 10, 2014. As of February 5, 2018:
http://www.govexec.com/excellence/promising-practices/2014/12/dont-run-pentagon/100917/

Nahrgang, Jennifer D., Frederick P. Morgeson, and David A. Hofman, "Safety at Work: A Meta-Analytic Investigation of the Link Between Job Demands, Job Resources, Burnout, Engagement, and Safety Outcomes," *Journal of Applied Psychology*, Vol. 96, No. 1, 2011, pp. 71–94.

National Commission on the Future of the Army, *Report to the President and the Congress of the United States*, Washington, D.C.: Government Printing Office, 2016.

NCFA—*See* National Commission on the Future of the Army.

Netenmeyer, Richard G., James S. Boles, and Robert McMurrian, "Development and Validation of Work-Family Conflict and Family-Work Conflict Scales," *Journal of Applied Psychology*, Vol. 81, No. 4, 1996, pp. 400–410.

Ng, T. W. H., and D. C. Feldman, "The Moderating Effects of Age in the Relationships of Job Autonomy to Work Outcomes," *Work, Aging, and Retirement*, Vol. 1, 2015, pp. 64–78.

Northcraft, Gregory B., Aaron M. Schmidt, and Susan J. Ashford, "Feedback and the Rationing of Time and Effort Among Competing Tasks," *Journal of Applied Psychology*, Vol. 96, No. 5, 2011, pp. 1076–1086.

NotBenedictArnold, "Battalion Commander's List of Number One Priorities Hits 50," *Duffle Blog*, June 15, 2017.
https://www.duffelblog.com/2017/06/battalion-commander-priorities/

Nowak, Jeff, "Base Evaluations on Professional Performance," *Proceedings Magazine*, October 2001, p. 94.

Oettingen, Gabriele, Heather Barry Kappes, Katie B. Guttenberg, and Peter M. Gollwitzer, "Self-Regulation of Time Management: Mental Contrasting with Implementation Intentions," *European Journal of Social Psychology*, Vol. 45, pp. 218–229.

Oldham, G. R., "Job Design," *International Review of Industrial and Organizational Psychology*, Vol. 11, 1996, pp. 33–60.

Olson, Taz, "Simply Not Enough Time: Time Management Is Needed," *Marine Corps Gazette*, Vol. 93, No. 10, October 2009, pp. 54–58.

Oncken, William, Jr., and Donald L. Wass, "Management Time: Who's Got the Monkey?" *Harvard Business Review*, November–December 1999, pp. 178–186.

"Opinions on SHARP Training," *RallyPoint.com*, November 8, 2013. As of February 5, 2018:
https://www.rallypoint.com/answers/opinions-on-sharp-training?loc=similar_mainandpos=0andtype=qrc

O'Reilly, Charles A., III, and Michael L. Tushman, "Ambidexterity as a Dynamic Capability: Resolving the Innovator's Dilemma," *Research in Organizational Behavior*, Vol. 28, 2008, pp. 185–206.

Orpen, Christopher, "The Effect of Time-Management Training on Employee Attitudes and Behavior: A Field Experiment," *The Journal of Psychology*, Vol. 128, No. 4, 1993, pp. 393–396.

Pache, Anne-Claire, and Filipe Santos, "When Worlds Collide: The Internal Dynamics of Organizational Responses to Conflicting Institutional Demands," *Academy of Management Review*, Vol. 35, No. 3, 2010, pp. 455–476.

Park, Nansook, Christopher Peterson, and Martin E. P. Seligman, "Strengths of Character and Well-Being," *Journal of Social and Clinical Psychology*, Vol. 23, No. 5, 2004, pp. 603–619.

Parker, Sharon, and Toby Wall, *Job and Work Design*, London, U.K.: Sage, 1999.

———, "Work Design: Learning from the Past and Mapping a New Terrain," in N. Anderson, D. S. Ones, H. K. Sinangil, and C. Viswesvaran, eds., *Handbook of Industrial, Work and Organizational Psychology*, Vol. 1, London, U.K.: Sage, 2001.

Parker, Sharon K., "Longitudinal Effects of Lean Production on Employee Outcomes and the Mediating Role of Work Characteristics," *Journal of Applied Psychology*, Vol. 88, 2003, pp. 620–634.

———, "Beyond Motivation: Job and Work Design for Development, Health, Ambidexterity, and More," *Annual Review of Psychology*, Vol. 65, 2014, pp. 661–691.

Pavluk, Joshua, and August Cole, "From Strategy to Execution: Accelerating the Third Offset," *War on the Rocks*, June 9, 2016. As of February 5, 2018: https://warontherocks.com/2016/06/from-strategy-to-execution-accelerating -the-third-offset/

Pearson, Kenneth O., III., "Bringing Combat Engineers Back to the Infantry," *Marine Corps Gazette*, Vol. 100, No. 10, October 2016, pp. 57–58.

Penttila, Chris, "Time Out," *Entrepreneur*, April 2007, pp. 70–73.

Perlow, Leslie, "Manage Your Team's Collective Time," *Harvard Business Review*, June 2014, pp. 23–25.

Petrou, Paraskevas, Evangelia Demerouti, Maria C. W. Peeters, Wilmar B. Schaufeli, and Jørn Hetland, "Crafting a Job on a Daily Basis: Contextual Correlates and the Link to Work Engagement," *Journal of Organizational Behavior*, Vol. 33, 2012, pp. 1120–1141.

Phillips, Steven R., "The New Time Management," *Training and Development Journal*, April 1988, pp. 73–77.

Pink, Daniel, *WHEN: The Scientific Secrets of Perfect Timing*, read by Daniel Pink, New York: Penguin Random House Audio, January 9, 2018.

Popov, Christo, "Why Your Employee Training Is a Waste of Time and Money— and What to Do About It," *Forbes*, August 30, 2015. As of February 5, 2018: https://www.forbes.com/sites/groupthink/2015/08/30/why-your-employee -training-is-a-waste-of-time-and-money-and-what-to-do-about-it/#6e23eda828cf

Post, Tom, "Entrepreneurs Clinic," *Forbes*, Vol. 19, No. 8, June 10, 2013.

Pratt, John R., "Time Management: 'The Hurrier I Go, the Behinder I Get,'" *Home Health Care Management and Practice*, Vol. 12, No. 4, 2000, pp. 61–63.

Probst, Tahira M., "Layoffs and Tradeoffs: Production, Quality, and Safety Demands Under the Threat of Job Loss," *Journal of Occupational Health Psychology*, Vol. 7, No. 3, 2002, pp. 211–220.

Purvanova, R. K., J. E. Bono, and J. Dzieweczynski, "Transformational Leadership, Job Characteristics, and Organizational Citizenship Performance," *Human Performance*, Vol. 19, 2006, pp. 1–22.

Raisch, Kelly, "Ten Pounds in a Five-Pound Bag: The Prescriptive and Overburdening Training Requirements for Today's Marines," *Marine Corps Gazette*, Vol. 97, No. 9, September 2013, pp. 75–77.

RallyPoint Team, "The GI Bill: How to Be Successful in School Pt. 4," *RallyPoint .com*, August 26, 2014. As of February 5, 2018: https://www.rallypoint.com/command-post/the-gi-bill-how-to-be-successful-in -school-pt-4

Ramesh, Balasubramaniam, Kannan Mohan, and Lan Cao, "Ambixeterity in Agile Distributed Development: An Empirical Investigation," *Information Systems Research*, Vol. 23, No. 2, 2012, pp. 323–339.

Ready, David, "Personnel Changes Required," *Marine Corps Gazette*, Vol. 99, No. 10, October 2015, pp. 40–42.

"Recruiters Overwhelmed," *Air Force Times*, September 8, 2014, p. 18.

Rhee, Seung-Yoon, Won-Moo Hur, and Minsung Kim, "The Relationship of Coworker Incivility to Job Performance and the Moderating Role of Self-Efficacy and Compassion at Work: The Job Demands-Resources (JD-R) Approach," *Journal of Business Psychology*, Vol. 32, No. 6, December 2017, pp. 711–726. As of July 15, 2019: https://doi.org/10.1007/s10869-016-9469-2

Riposo, Jessie, Brien Alkire, John F. Schank, Mark V. Arena, James G. Kallimani, Irv Blickstein, Kimberly Curry Hall, and Clifford A. Grammich, *U.S. Navy Shipyards: An Evaluation of Workload- and Workforce-Management Practices*, Santa Monica, Calif.: RAND Corporation, MG-751-NAVY, 2008. As of July 15, 2019: https://www.rand.org/pubs/monographs/MG751.html

Roberts, K. H., and W. Glick, "The Job Characteristics Approach to Job Design: A Critical Review," *Journal of Applied Psychology*, Vol. 66, 1981, pp. 193–217.

Robinson, Donald J., II., "There Is Not Enough Time" (letter to the editor), *Marine Corps Gazette*, November 2013, p. 5.

Rockwood, Kate, "Endless Meetings? Your Schedule Can Be Tamed," *Inc.*, June 2017, p. 40.

Roethlisberger, F. J., and W. J. Dickson, *Management and the Worker*, Boston, Mass.: Harvard University Press, 1939.

Rose, Judy, "Never Enough Hours in the Day: Employed Mothers' Perceptions of Time Pressure," *Australian Journal of Social Issues*, Vol. 52, 2017, pp. 116–130.

Rue, W. Jonathan, "DoD Civilians: Cutting the Workforce but Not the Workload," *War on the Rocks*, August 4, 2015. As of February 5, 2018: https://warontherocks.com/2015/08/dod-civilians-cutting-the-workforce-but-not -the-workload/

Russell, Cary B., *DOD Training: DOD Has Taken Steps to Assess Common Military Training*, Washington, D.C.: U.S. Government Accountability Office, GAO-17-468, 2017.

Ruvolo, Catherine M., and R. Craig Bullis, "Essentials of Culture Change: Lessons Learned the Hard Way," *Consulting Psychology Journal: Practice and Research*, Vol. 55, No. 3, 2003, pp. 155–168.

Salancik, G. R., and J. Pfeffer, "An Examination of Need Satisfaction Models of Job Attitudes," *Administrative Science Quarterly*, Vol. 22, 1977, pp. 427–456.

———, "A Social Information Processing Approach to Job Attitudes and Task Design," *Administrative Science Quarterly*, Vol. 23, 1978, pp. 224–253.

Schafer, Amy, "Why Military Personnel Reform Matters," *War on the Rocks*, October 29, 2015. As of February 5, 2018: https://warontherocks.com/2015/10/why-military-personnel-reform-matters/

Schaufeli, W. B., M. P. Leiter, C. Maslach, and S. E. Jackson, "Maslach Burnout Inventory—General Survey (MBI–GS)," in C. A. Maslach, S. E. Jackson, and M. P. Leiter, eds., *Maslach Burnout Inventory Manual*, 3rd ed., Palo Alto, Calif.: Consulting Psychologists Press, 1996.

Schaufeli, W. B., M. Salanova, V. Gonzalez-Roma, and A. B. Bakker, "The Measurement of Engagement and Burnout: A Two Sample Confirmatory Factor Analytic Approach," *Journal of Happiness Studies*, Vol. 3, 2002, pp. 71–92.

Schaufeli, W. B., and Toon W. Taris, "A Critical Review of the Job Demands-Resources Model: Implications for Improving Work and Health," in G. F. Bauer and O. Hämmig, eds., *Bridging Occupational, Organizational and Public Health: A Transdisciplinary Approach*, Dordrecht, the Netherlands: Springer, 2014, pp. 43–68.

Schlosser, Julie, "Nandan Nikelani," *Forbes International (Europe)*, Vol. 153, No. 3, March 20, 2006, p. 47.

Schrage, Michael, "I Know What You Mean. And I Can't Do Anything About It," *Fortune*, Vol. 143, No. 7, April 2, 2001, p. 186.

Schmidt, Aaron M., James W. Beck, and Jennifer Z. Gilespie, "Motivation," in Neal W. Schmitt, Scott Highhouse, and Irving B. Weiner, eds., *Handbook of Psychology*, Vol. 12: *Industrial and Organizational Psychology*, 2nd ed., Hoboken, N.J.: Wiley, 2013, pp. 311–340.

Schmidt, Aaron M., and Richard P. DeShon, "What to Do? The Effects of Discrepancies, Incentives, and Time on Dynamic Goal Prioritization," *Journal of Applied Psychology*, Vol. 92, 2007, pp. 928–941.

Schmidt, Aaron M., and Chad M. Dolis, "Something's Got to Give: The Effects of Dual-Goal Difficulty, Goal Progress, and Expectancies on Resource Allocation," *Journal of Applied Psychology*, Vol. 94, 2009, pp. 678–691.

Scott, Ryan, "Willful Disobedience: Character Traits of Independent Thinkers in the Military," *Mwi.usma.edu: Commentary & Analysis*, February 23, 2017. As of February 15, 2018: https://mwi.usma.edu/willful-disobedience-character-traits-independent-thinkers-military/

Sellers, Patricia, "A Double Shot of Productivity," *Fortune*, Vol. 154, No. 8, October 16, 2006, p. 51.

Seligman, Martin E. P., Tracy A. Steen, Nansook Park, and Christopher Peterson, "Positive Psychology Progress: Empirical Validation of Interventions," *American Psychologist*, Vol. 60, No. 5, 2005, pp. 410–421.

Shabatary, Dvir, George Steiner, and Rui Zhang, "Optimal Coordination of Resource Allocation, Due Date Assignment and Scheduling Decisions," *Omega*, Vol. 65, December 2016, pp. 41–54.

Shane, Leo, III, "Congress Is Giving the Officer Promotion System a Massive Overhaul," *Military Times*, July 25, 2018. As of July 15, 2019:
https://www.militarytimes.com/news/your-military/2018/07/25/how-officers-are
-promoted-will-get-its-biggest-overhaul-in-decades-heres-what-that-means-for
-the-military/

Shipp, A. J., J. R. Edwards, and L. S. Lambert, "Conceptualization and Measurement of Temporal Focus: The Subjective Experience of the Past, Present, and Future," *Organizational Behavior and Human Decision Processes*, Vol. 110, No. 1, 2009, pp. 1–22.

Sims, Carra S., Thomas E. Trail, Emily K. Chen, Erika Meza, Parisa Roshan, and Beth E. Lachman, *Assessing the Needs of Soldiers and Their Families at the Garrison Level*, Santa Monica, Calif.: RAND Corporation, RR-2148-A, 2017. As of July 15, 2019:
https://www.rand.org/pubs/research_reports/RR2148.html

Smith, Adam, *An Inquiry into the Nature and Causes of the Wealth of Nations*, London, Great Britain: W. Strahan and T. Cadell, 1776.

Spears, William, "A Case for Results-Based Training," *U.S. Naval Institute Blog*, July 19, 2013. As of February 5, 2018:
https://blog.usni.org/posts/2013/07/19/a-case-for-results-based-training

Spector, P. E., "A Consideration of the Validity and Meaning of Self-Report Measures of Job Conditions," in C. L. Cooper and I. T. Robertson, eds., *International Review of Industrial and Organizational Psychology*, Vol. 7, New York: Wiley, 1992, pp. 123–151.

Spector, P. E., and S. M. Jex, "Relations of Job Characteristics from Multiple Data Sources with Employee Affect, Absence, Turnover Intentions, and Health," *Journal of Applied Psychology*, Vol. 76, 1991, pp. 46–53.

Stajkovic, Alexander D., and Fred Luthans, "Self-Efficacy and Work-Related Performance: A Meta-Analysis," *Psychological Bulletin*, Vol. 124, No. 2, pp. 240–261.

Stone, Teresa Elizabeth, and Anna Elizabeth Teloar, "'How Did It Get So Late So Soon?': Tips and Tricks for Managing Time," *Nursing and Health Sciences*, Vol. 17, 2015, pp. 409–411.

Strickland, Oriel J., and Mark Galimba, "Managing Time: The Effects of Personal Goal Setting on Resource Allocation Strategy and Task Performance," *The Journal of Psychology*, Vol. 135, No. 4, 2001, pp. 357–367.

Stubbs, Paul, "Infantry Officer: Blowing off Orders Has Become a Troubling Norm," *Marine Corps Times*, March 13, 2016.

Taylor, F. W., *The Principles of Scientific Management*, New York: Norton, 1911.

Terborg, J. R., and G. A. Davis, "Evaluation of a New Method for Assessing Change to Planned Job Redesign as Applied to Hackman and Oldham's Job Characteristic Model," *Organizational Behavior and Human Performance*, Vol. 29, 1982, pp. 112–128.

Tiegs, R. B., L. E. Tetrick, and Y. Fried, "Growth Need Strength and Context Satisfactions as Moderators of the Relations of the Job Characteristics Model," *Journal of Management*, Vol. 18, 1992, pp. 575–593.

Tims, Maria, Arnold B. Bakker, and D. Derks, "Development and Validation of the Job Crafting Scale," *Journal of Vocational Behavior*, Vol. 80, 2012, pp. 173–186.

Trimailo, Timothy, "Epic Fail: Why Leaders Must Fail to Ultimately Succeed," *Military Review*, November–December 2017. As of July 15, 2019: https://www.armyupress.army.mil/Journals/Military-Review/English-Edition -Archives/November-December-2017/Epic-Fail-Why-Leaders-Must-Fail-to -Ultimately-Succeed/

Trist, E. L., and K. M. Bamforth, "Some Social and Psychological Consequences of the Longwall Method of Coal-Getting," *Human Relations*, Vol. 4, 1951, pp. 3–38.

Unger, Dana, Cornelia Niessen, Sabine Sonnentag, and Angela Neff, "A Question of Time: Daily Time Allocation Between Work and Private Life," *Journal of Occupational and Organizational Psychology*, Vol. 87, 2014, pp. 158–176.

U.S. Army Forces Command, *FORSCOM Command Training Guidance Fiscal Year 2017*, Fort Bragg, N.C., 2016.

———, *FORSCOM Command Training Guidance Fiscal Year 2018*, Fort Bragg, N.C., 2017.

U.S. Army Inspector General Agency, *Report of the Disciplined Leadership and Company Administrative Requirements Inspection*, Washington, D.C.: U.S. Department of Defense, February 2, 2012.

U.S. Census Bureau, *American Time Use Survey User's Guide: Understanding ATUS 2003 to 2017*, Washington, D.C.: U.S. Bureau of Labor Statistics, June 2018. As of July 15, 2019: https://www.bls.gov/tus/atususersguide.pdf

U.S. Department of the Army, *Field Manual 5-0: The Operations Process*, Washington, D.C.: U.S. Army, 2010.

———, G-3/5/7 Staff, "National Commission on the Future of the Army: Enable, Resource, Build, Assess, and Sustain Training Readiness," briefing slides, Fort Bragg, N.C.: U.S. Army Forces Command, September 17, 2015.

———, *Field Manual 7-0: Train to Win in a Complex World*, Washington, D.C.: U.S. Army, 2016.

U.S. Government Accountability Office, *Defense Management: DOD Needs to Address Inefficiencies and Implement Reform Across Its Defense Agencies and DOD Field Activities*, Washington, D.C.: U.S. GAO, GAO-18-592, September 2018. As of July 15, 2019:
https://www.gao.gov/products/GAO-18-592

Van Den Broeck, Anja, Nele De Cuyper, Hans De Witte, and Maarten Vansteenkiste, "Not All Job Demands Are Equal: Differentiating Job Hindrances and Job Challenges in the Job Demands-Resources Model," *European Journal of Work and Organizational Psychology*, Vol. 19, No. 6, 2010, pp. 735–759.

Vandergriff, Donald E. "Building Adaptive Leaders: The Army Can Adapt Its Institution (Pt. 1)," *Small Wars Journal*, 2008.

Van Dun, Desiree H., Jeff N. Nicks, and Celeste P. M. Wilderom, "Values and Behaviors of Effective Lean Managers: Mixed-Methods Exploratory Research," *European Management Journal*, Vol. 35, 2017, pp. 174–186.

Van Dyne, L., and S. Ang, "Organizational Citizenship Behavior of Contingent Workers in Singapore," *Academy of Management Journal*, Vol. 41, 1998, pp. 692–703.

Van Eerde, Wendelien, "Procrastination at Work and Time Management Training," *The Journal of Psychology*, Vol. 137, No. 5, 2003, pp. 421–434.

Van Horn, Mark, "Afternoon PT: Key for an Army Flextime Battle Rhythm," *Military Review*, Vol. 89, No. 5, 2009, pp. 72–79.

Van Wingerden, Jessica, Arnold B. Bakker, and Daantje Derks, "The Longitudinal Impact of a Job Crafting Intervention," *European Journal of Work and Organizational Psychology*, Vol. 26, No. 1, 2017, pp. 107–119.

Van Woerkom, M., A. B. Bakker, and L. H. Nishii, "Accumulative Job Demands and Support for Strength Use: Fine-Tuning the Job Demands-Resources Model Using Conservation of Resources Theory," *Journal of Applied Psychology*, Vol. 101, 2016, pp. 141–150.

Vesilind, Emili, "The Home Office Is Humming," *Entrepreneur*, June 2010, pp. 98–103.

Vestal, K. W., "Job Design: Process and Product," *Nursing Management*, Vol. 20, 1989, pp. 26–29.

Vistisen, Hiels Klingenberg, "The Missing Operational Level: COIN, Afghanistan, and IJC," *Small Wars Journal*, 2012.

Waldum, Emily R., and Mark A. McDaniel, "Why Are You Late? Investigating the Role of Time Management in Time-Based Prospective Memory," *Journal of Experimental Psychology: General*, Vol. 145, No. 8, 2016, pp. 1049–1061.

Wall, T. D., and P. R. Jackson, "Changes in Manufacturing and Shopfloor Job Design," in A. Howard, ed., *The Changing Nature of Work*, San Francisco, Calif.: Jossey-Bass, 1995, pp. 164–211.

Waller, Mary J., Jeffrey M. Conte, Cristina B. Gibson, and Mason A. Carpenter, "The Effect of Individual Perceptions of Deadlines on Team Performance," *Academy of Management Review*, Vol. 26, No. 4, October 2001, pp. 586–600.

Waller, Mary J., Mary E. Zellmer-Bruhn, and Robert C. Giambatista, "Watching the Clock: Group Pacing Behavior Under Dynamic Deadlines," *Academy of Management Journal*, Vol. 45, No. 5, 2002, pp. 1046–1055.

Ward, M., *The National Incident Management Command System Field Guide*, 2nd ed., Tigard, Oreg.: Informed Publishing, 2007.

"Ways to Build a Better List," *Health*, Vol. 17, No. 1, January–February 2003, p. 162.

Wesman, Jane, "The Simplest System," *Inc.*, Vol. 18, No. 12, September 1996, p. 109.

"What NOT to Do as a Platoon Leader," *ARMY Magazine*, December 2013, pp. 53–57.

Whittinghill, Craig, David Berkowitz, and Phillip A. Farrington, "Does Your Culture Encourage Innovation?" *Defense Acquisition Research Journal*, Vol. 22, No. 2, April 2015, pp. 216–239.

Witkowski, Mary, "5 Things It Will Take to Keep Working Mothers Like Me in the Navy," *U.S. Naval Institute Blog*, July 14, 2015. As of February 5, 2018: https://blog.usni.org/posts/2015/07/14/5-things-it-will-take-to-keep-working-mothers-like-me-in-the-navy

Wolter, Romanus, "Kick Back and Relax," *Entrepreneur*, September 2004.

———, "Trust Your Team," *Entrepreneur*, November 2006, p. 152.

Wong, Leonard, *Stifled Innovation? Developing Tomorrow's Leaders Today*, Carlisle Barracks, Pa.: U.S. Army War College Strategic Studies Institute, 2002.

Wong, Leonard, and Stephen J. Gerras, *Lying to Ourselves: Dishonesty in the Army Profession*, Carlisle Barracks, Pa.: Strategic Studies Institute and U.S. Army War College Press, 2015.

Woody, Christopher, "Mattis and U.S. Military Leaders Are Trying to Get Rid of the Worst Parts of Military Service," *Business Insider*, July 26, 2007. As of February 5, 2018:
http://www.businessinsider.com/mattis-military-leaders-to-reduce-training-and-administrative-duties-2017-7

Wright, B. M., and J. L. Cordery, "Production Uncertainty as a Contextual Moderator of Employee Reactions to Job Design," *Journal of Applied Psychology*, Vol. 84, 1999, pp. 456–463.

Wrzesniewski, Amy, and Jane E. Dutton, "Crafting a Job: Revisioning Employee as Active Crafters of Their Work," *Academy of Management Review*, Vol. 26, 2001, pp. 179–201.

Xanthopoulou, Despoina, Arnold B. Bakker, Evangelia Demerouti, and Wilmar B. Schaufeli, "The Role of Personal Resources in the Job Demands-Resources Model," *International Journal of Stress Management*, Vol. 14, No. 2, 2007, pp. 121–141.

Xu, Jianzhong, Ruiping Yuan, Brian Xu, and Melinda Xu, "Modeling Students' Time Management in Math Homework," *Learning and Individual Differences*, Vol. 34, 2014, pp. 33–42.

Yardley, Roland J., Dulani Woods, Cesse Cameron Ip, and Jerry M. Sollinger, *General Military Training: Standardization and Reduction Options*, Santa Monica, Calif.: RAND Corporation, TR-1222-OSD, 2012. As of February 5, 2018:
https://www.rand.org/pubs/technical_reports/TR1222.html

Yau, Nathan, "Counting the Hours," *FlowingData*, undated. As of July 31, 2019:
https://flowingdata.com/2015/11/10/counting-the-hours/

Yoels, William C., and Jeffrey Michael Clair, "Never Enough Time: How Medical Residents Manage a Scarce Resource," *Journal of Contemporary Ethnography*, Vol. 23, No. 2, 1994, pp. 185–213.

Ziezulewicz, Geoff, "McCain: 20 Sailors Reprimanded in the Wake of 7th Fleet At-Sea Incidents," *Navy Times*, September 19, 2017a. As of February 5, 2018:
https://www.navytimes.com/news/your-navy/2017/09/19/sen-mccain-20-sailors-reprimanded-in-wake-of-summers-fatal-at-sea-collisions/

———, "No Rest for the Weary: Lack of Sleep Threatens Safety and Readiness," *Navy Times*, September 19, 2017b. As of February 5, 2018:
https://www.navytimes.com/news/your-navy/2017/09/19/no-rest-for-the-weary-lack-of-sleep-threatens-safety-and-readiness/

Żołnierczyk-Zreda, Dorota, "An Intervention to Reduce Work-Related Burnout in Teachers," *International Journal of Occupational Safety and Ergonomics*, Vol. 11, No. 4, 2005, pp. 423–430.